THE PICTORIAL HISTORY OF
BASKETBALL

BILL GUTMAN

GALLERY BOOKS
An imprint of W.H. Smith Publishers Inc.
112 Madison Avenue
New York, New York 10016

A Bison Book

Published by Gallery Books
A Division of W H Smith Publishers Inc.
112 Madison Avenue
New York, New York 10016

Produced by
Bison Books Corp.
15 Sherwood Place
Greenwich, CT 06830

ISBN 0-8317-6888-6

Printed in Spain

10 9 8 7 6 5 4 3 2 1

PAGE 1: Photo by Mike Rose.

PAGES 2-3: Insets left to right: Coach
Adolph Rupp (Photo courtesy The Edward J
and Gena G Hickox Library, Naismith
Memorial Basketball Hall of Fame); Pete
Maravich of the Atlanta Hawks (Malcolm W
Emmons Photo); George Mikan of the
Minneapolis Lakers (UPI/Bettmann
Newsphotos); UCLA Bruins' Lew Alcindor
(Malcolm W Emmons Photo); Purdue's Mark
Aguirre (Malcolm W Emmons Photo).
Background photo: A 1981 NCAA game in
Philadelphia (Malcolm W Emmons photo).

PICTURE CREDITS

The Bettmann Archive, Inc:
    pages 6, 9(bottom),
    11(bottom), 13, 20(both),
    145(top).
The Edward J and Gena G
    Hickox Library, Naismith
    Memorial Basketball Hall of
    Fame: pages 7(both), 8(top),
    10, 11(top), 12, 16(bottom),
    17(both), 18, 19, 21, 27(left),
    38, 41, 49(bottom),
    51(bottom), 52, 64(top), 65,
    78(bottom), 79, 80(right),
    97, 130, 132, 135, 136,
    137(both), 138, 139(both),
    141(left), 142(both), 143,146,
    147(right), 153(top),
    155(both), 159(top), 160,
    162(bottom), 163,
    165(bottom), 166, 168, 170,
    176, 178, 179, 182.
Malcolm W Emmons: pages
    76(both), 77(top), 78,
    80(left), 81, 83(top & bottom
    left), 86-87(all three), 88,
    89(both), 90, 91, 92,
    93(both), 94(both), 95,
    96(both), 98(both), 99(both),
    100, 101(both), 102(all four),
    103(both), 104, 105, 106,
    107, 108(bottom), 109, 110,
    111(both), 112(both), 113(all
    four), 114(both), 115, 116,
    117, 118, 119, 120, 121, 122,
    123, 124, 125(both),
    126(both), 127, 128(both),
    129, 180, 183, 184,
    186(both), 187, 188(both),
    189(all three), 190, 191,
    192(both), 193, 194(both),
    195, 196, 197, 198, 199, 200,
    201(both), 202(all three),
    203, 204, 205(both), 206.
UPI/Bettmann Newsphotos:
    pages 14, 22, 23(both), 24,
    25(both), 26, 27(right), 28,
    29, 30, 31, 32, 33, 34(both),
    35(both), 36-37, 39, 40, 42,
    43(both), 44(both), 45,
    46-47, 47, 48, 49(top), 50,
    51(top), 53(both), 54, 55, 56,
    57, 58(both), 59(both), 60-
    61(all three) 62, 63(both),
    64(bottom), 66, 66-67, 68,
    69, 70, 71(both),72, 73, 74,
    75(both), 82, 83(bottom
    right), 84(both), 86,
    108(top), 133, 134, 140,
    141(right) 144, 145(bottom),
    147(left), 148, 149, 150, 151,
    152, 153(bottom), 154, 156,
    157, 158, 159(bottom), 161,
    162(top), 164(both), 165(top),
    166-67, 169(both), 171(both),
    172, 173, 174(both), 175,
    177, 178, 179, 181, 185.
Yale Sports Publicity: page
    16(top)

ACKNOWLEDGMENTS

The author and publisher
    would like to thank the
    following people who helped
    in the preparation of this
    book: John Kirk, who edited
    it; Donna Cornell Muntz,
    who did the picture
    research; Design 23, who
    designed it; and Cynthia
    Klein, who prepared the
    index.

CONTENTS

*After leaving Springfied,
James Naismith moved on
to Kansas University,
where he continued to
spread the word about his
new game. Here the
inventor of basketball
shows Marcella Morewitz,
left, and Grace Endicott the
fine points of the center
jump.*

PART I

The Origins of Basketball

IN THE BEGINNING

Basketball may be the only major sport that came into being as the direct result of a request. There was no evolution, no gradual crystallizing of a sport from a loosely connected group of physical activities. On the contrary, basketball may be the greatest example of invent-a-sport that ever was.

The request came from Dr Luther Gulick, the head of the physical education department of the International Training School of the Young Men's Christian Association in Springfield, Massachusetts. In the autumn of 1891 Dr Gulick saw a problem at the Training School, which would later become Springfield College. He felt that the young men at the school just weren't interested in the traditional cold-weather indoor activities such as marching, gymnastics and calisthenics. After pondering over this problem for a time Dr Gulick turned to a 30-year-old physical education instructor at the school, James Naismith. He remembered a previous conversation with Naismith in which the younger man talked of inventing a new game that could be played indoors. So he asked Naismith to take over the physical education class and think about coming up with that new game.

James Naismith was a native of Canada, having been born in Almonte, Ontario, and educated at McGill University, where he studied for the ministry for three years before deciding that he was better suited to physical education. That decision made, he came to the Springfield school and, after graduation, became an instructor. Upon taking over the physical education class at the Training School, Naismith quickly confirmed what Dr Gulick had told him. The students were bored, even downright rebellious. It wasn't long before he stopped the gymnastics and calisthenics and tried to concentrate on games. But those games with which he was already familiar quickly proved unsuited for play indoors and on a hard gymnasium floor.

He tried rugby, for instance, but the hard tackling made the game too rough for the indoor arena. Soccer was similarly unsuitable. In the confined area the players kicked each other and proceeded to break the windows in the gym when they really connected with the ball. Lacrosse, too, was a disaster. When tempers flared the players would begin using their sticks as clubs.

Naismith was temporarily stumped and even thought about telling Dr Gulick he couldn't handle the assignment. Then he began to think about a new game. How about something with a large round ball, he thought. That way, the players wouldn't need any kind of sticks, rackets or similar equipment. But what to do with the ball? If the players ran with it, the game would quickly deteriorate into mayhem. No, there had to be some way to move it. Perhaps throwing it was the answer. But throwing it where? And to what purpose?

After giving the subject much thought Naismith concluded that the ball would have to be thrown into or through some kind of goal. If the goal was up high, he figured, and the ball had to be arched, he could eliminate

OPPOSITE FAR LEFT: *Dr Luther Gulick was the man who actually asked James Naismith to invent a new sport. Dr Gulick didn't know what his young protege would finally devise, but didn't complain when Naismith laid out the ground rules for basketball.*

OPPOSITE LEFT: *Before he invented the court game, the burly Naismith was a football player who fully looked the part of a young athlete of his time.*

ABOVE: *This gymnasium at the School for Christian Workers was full of 19th century athletic gear. It was also the site of the first basketball game, played in December 1891.*

RIGHT: *It didn't take long before illustrators became aware of the new sport. This drawing depicts the first basketball game, with peach basket and someone to retrieve the ball after each basket.*

still another source of possible injury. He seemed on the way to designing a kind of finesse game. Perhaps he was on the right track after all.

That night James Naismith wrote down his original rules for the game. The next day he went to the gym to try to set the game up. He asked a janitor if he had any kind of boxes that could be used as goals. All the man had was a pair of peach baskets. They would have to do. Naismith himself nailed them up to the balcony that surrounded the gym. He put one at each end at a height of exactly ten feet. And when his gym class arrived that day James Naismith introduced them to the new game, a game in which a team scored when

it was able to put the ball through the peach basket. So in mid-December of 1891 basketball was officially born.

It wasn't until January 1892, when the students came back to school from their Christmas vacation, that Naismith posted the first set of rules written for the new game. This is exactly what the training school boys read about the game with the round ball and the two peach baskets.

1. The ball may be thrown in any direction with one or both hands.
2. The ball may be batted in any direction with one or both hands (never with the fist).

9

3. A player cannot run with the ball. The player must throw it from the spot on which he catches it, allowance to be made for a man who catches the ball when running if he tries to stop.

4. The ball must be held in or between the hands; the arms or body must not be used for holding it.

5. No shouldering, holding, pushing, tripping or striking in any way the person of any opponent shall be allowed; the first infringement of this rule by any person shall count as a foul, the second shall disqualify him until the next goal is made, or if there was evident intent to injure the person, for the whole of the game, no substitute allowed.

6. A foul is striking at the ball with the fist, violations of Rules 3, 4 and such as described in Rule 5.

7. If either side makes three consecutive fouls, it shall count as a goal for the opponents (consecutive means without the opponents in the mean time making a foul).

8. A goal shall be made when the ball is thrown or batted from the ground into the basket and stays there, providing those defending the goal do not touch or disturb the goal. If the ball rests on the edges, and an opponent moves the basket, it shall count as a goal.

9. When the ball goes out of bounds, it shall be thrown into the field and played by the person first touching it. He has a right to hold it unmolested for five seconds. In case of a dispute the umpire shall throw it straight into the field. The thrower-in is allowed five seconds; if he holds it longer it shall go to the opponent. If any side persists in delaying the game the umpire shall call a foul on that side.

10. The umpire shall be the judge of the men and shall note the fouls and notify the referee when three consecutive fouls have been made. He shall have the power to disqualify men according to Rule 5.

11. The referee shall be the judge of the ball and shall decide when the ball is in play, in bounds, to which side it belongs and shall keep the time. He shall decide when a goal has been made and keep account of the goals, with any other duties that are usually performed by a referee.

12. The time shall be two fifteen-minute halves, with five minutes rest between.

13. The side making the most goals in that time shall be declared the winners. In the case of a draw the game may, by agreement of the captains, be continued until another goal is made.

Today's game is barely recognizable from Naismith's 13 original rules. There is no mention of dribbling, for instance, though Naismith had already decided to put the ball in play by tossing it in the air between two players: That would eventually become the center jump. He had also decided on five seconds as the amount of time a player had to throw the ball in play. That rule is still in existence today.

The way Naismith envisioned the game originally, it would be played with nine men on a side. Within a year, there was a provision for a five-man game in small gymnasiums, and for the next several years the game was played with five, seven or nine, depending on the size of the gym. Finally, in 1897, five men on a side became the official norm for the new sport.

As for the name, someone had suggested that the game be called Naismith-ball. But the inventor would not hear of that. When someone suggested basketball, the logical result of having to put the ball into the basket, everyone agreed. Basketball it would be, and basketball it has remained.

The new game spread quickly. The first games were played early in 1892, and by that time the newspaper at the International Training School had published an article describing basketball which was distributed to all the YMCA's throughout the world. Even the *New York Times*

LEFT: *Dr Naismith with his first basketball team at the YMCA Training School in Springfield in December of 1891. Naismith is wearing the suit in the middle row. The others are names now largely forgotten.*

OPPOSITE ABOVE: *The ladies also took to basketball in the early days. The first woman's game was played between Smith College students in Northampton, Mass, in March of 1893. Here Senda Berenson (in long dress) is set to toss the ball for the center jump as the other girls get ready. Their outfits are a far cry from the uniforms of today.*

OPPOSITE RIGHT: *Another turn-of-the-century ladies game being played in rather formal dress. Notice the old six-foot-wide foul lane and the "key." Most free throws were taken underhand then, and the basket was attached right to the gym wall, without a backboard.*

was writing about the sport as early as April 1892.

Naismith himself continued to work at spreading the game. He took the Training School team on the road to play a series of exhibitions, and by 1894 he said that the game was already being played to some extent worldwide. In addition, basketball was beginning to appear at the college level, and even two women's colleges, Vassar and Smith, added basketball to their list of physical activities as early as 1892.

In fact, when he first thought about the game, James Naismith envisioned it being played by women as well as men. As early as March 1892 a group of local Springfield women played against a team of woman teachers. Naismith was at that game and ultimately married one of the participants, Maude Sherman.

The inventor saw his game as one that the average man and woman would be comfortable playing. He certainly didn't envision it as a high-powered professional sport. But in a sense he was well aware of the type of game he had designed, for in describing what he considered the average player, he created a description that could well fit the great players of today.

"I had in mind the tall, agile, graceful and expert athlete," he wrote, "one who could reach, jump and act quickly and easily." If one didn't know better, it would almost seem as if Naismith was describing a Bill Russell or a Julius Erving.

Russell and Erving, of course, would come much later and would hardly have recognized the game of those first years. For instance, at the beginning, a field goal counted just a single point, and a team was also awarded a point when the opposing team committed three fouls. Later, field goals were worth three points, then within a short time dropped to two. The free throw also came into existence before too much time passed, and by 1897 the free throw line

was set at 15 feet from the hoop.

The first metal hoops were used instead of a peach basket as early as 1893, and by 1895 the backboard began to appear, although the game was still played here and there with a basket suspended atop a verticle pole. It would be a good number of years before the rules were really standarized.

And there were some concepts that just had to be changed. For instance, the original out of bounds play allowed the first player to touch the ball *after* it went out of bounds to throw it back in. That led to mad scrambles for the out-of-bounds ball, and with nine players on a side, it often got out of hand. Though the rule lasted for a number of years, it was finally changed for good around 1913, with today's rule stipulating that the team last touching the ball would lose possession. That definitely took some of the wildness and unnecessary roughness out of the game.

And while Naismith's original 13 rules did not mention the dribble, that was another addition that came quite soon. In fact, it more or less evolved in order to make the game flow better and allow for more skillful play. The original concept called for the ball to be moved only through passing. But sometimes a player was so closely guarded or even double-teamed that a pass was nearly impossible.

To compensate originally, a rule was added allowing the player to throw the ball into the air, then catch it again himself. In other words, he was throwing himself a pass. He was soon allowed a series of these passes, and before long the passes turned into bounces, and dribbling became the alternative to passing when advancing or moving the ball.

The early scores were, by today's standards, incredibly low. In 1896, for example, there was a YMCA tournament staged with the winner to be declared "Champion of America." In the final game, two Brooklyn teams played, and the East District defeated Brooklyn Central by a base-ball-like score of 4-0. It wasn't unusual in those early years to have games in which neither team could manage 10 points.

As for James Naismith, he left Springfield in 1895, just a little over three years after inventing his new game. But he never really left basketball. At first, he went to a YMCA in Colorado, and while working there he returned to school and became a medical doctor in 1898.

Yet he chose to remain in physical education. He was appointed head of the physical education department of the University of Kansas in 1898 and brought his passion for basketball with him. He coached the university team for nine years and remained a faculty member at the school until his retirement in 1937.

His interest in sports and physical fitness never left him.

LEFT: *This old print shows a rather young and formal James Naismith not looking anything like an athlete or the inventor of a new and rapidly growing sport. But Naismith remained involved with basketball until his death in 1939.*

OPPOSITE: *An older James Naismith always found time to show his son, James, the finer points of the game. Note the large laced ball.*

He himself was a burly man who, while standing just five feet, nine inches tall, weighed in the neighborhood of 200 pounds. His son, James S Naismith, once wrote that even in his father's later years, "I still would not have wanted to engage him in physical combat."

Dr James Naismith died in 1939 at the age of 78. He lived long enough to see his sport played extensively at the high school and college levels, and while the pro game was still struggling for stability then, and was not yet on a par with baseball, football or even hockey, Naismith knew there were men making money by playing his game.

One thing, however, is certain. If James Naismith were to see his sport today, a sport played in backyards and playgrounds everywhere, as well as in some of the world's greatest sports arenas, he undoubtedy would have smiled with pride at his baby all grown up and in its prime.

College players took the
game of basketball very
seriously from the
beginning. This fine City
College of New York team
of the late 1930s was no
exception. Under coach Nat
Holman, CCNY could
compete with anyone right
into the 1950s. Left to right
are Isadore Katz, Manny
Jarmon, Babe Adler, John
Foley, Dave Paris, Lou
Lefkowitz, Morris
Goldstein and captain
Bernard Fliegal.

PART 2

The College Game

EARLY YEARS

It should come as little or no surprise that basketball made a fairly rapid entrance into the world of college athletics. With the competitive nature of colleges and universities, as well as the academic world's inquisitiveness about anything new, there was an almost immediate reaction to the infant sport.

The game spread as a result of its initial acceptance at YMCAs throughout the country. And because nearly every college town had a Y, college students as well as coaches were soon exposed to the game. In fact, one of the early proponents of college basketball was none other than Amos Alonzo Stagg, a man usually associated with football. But Stagg was at the same YMCA training school in Springfield when James Naismith invented the game. He took to it quickly, like most of the others at the Y, and when he became the first athletic director and coach of the newly opened University of Chicago in the autumn of 1892, he brought thoughts of basketball to the windy city with him.

It wasn't long before Stagg had his students playing the game on an intramural level. He started a varsity team in 1894, but because no other area colleges played then, Stagg had to be content to send his team up against various local clubs from the area. The University of Chicago began playing other colleges in 1896, with its first and only opponent that year being the University of Iowa.

But Chicago wasn't the first college to start a basketball program. Thanks to another Springfield alumnus, Charles Bemies, basketball came to little Geneva College in Beaver Falls, Pennsylvania, as early as February 1892, just two years after the school began a football program.

Within a short time, other colleges were beginning to play the sport, either at the intramural level or against local

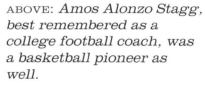

ABOVE: *Amos Alonzo Stagg, best remembered as a college football coach, was a basketball pioneer as well.*

LEFT: *An early University of Pennsylvania team reflects the style and dress of early 20th century basketball.*

OPPOSITE ABOVE: *One of the early versions of the game saw it played on grass with the basket suspended atop a straight pole.*

OPPOSITE RIGHT: *The honor of introducing basketball into college sport went to little Geneva College in Beaver Falls, Pennsylvania. This photo shows Geneva's first team, assembled in 1891. Standing, center, is team captain C O Bemies.*

culture defeated Hamline University of St Paul 9-3. And just a month later, Haverford College topped Temple in perhaps the first great upset in college hoop history. The score, 6-4. That's a long time between baskets.

But the 1894-95 season marked the real beginning of intercollegiate play. And not coincidentally, a number of those early programs were started by friends and former colleagues of Dr Naismith. Dr Henry Kallenberg, who started the Iowa program, knew both Naismith and Amos Stagg. Charles Williams, the organizer at Temple, had been a student of Naismith's at Springfield. And Ray Kaighn, who took part in the first collegiate game ever at Hamline, had also been one of Naismith's colleagues at Springfield.

A game between Chicago and Iowa in 1896 was the first contest between two colleges played with only five men on a side. And the second game that year produced the then unusually high score of 34-18. But there was very little structure or uniformity to the early game, and that sometimes caused problems.

Not all school or even town and YMCA teams had new gymnasiums in which to play, and teams often found themselves playing in halls with low ceilings or other inconveniences. The University of Pennsylvania actually dropped basketball for about a four-year period between 1898 and 1902 because the gym at the school had pillars on the court and that proved a danger to the players.

Yet the sport continued to grow at the turn of the century. It spread from Yale to Harvard, for example, when a Yale graduate named John Kirkland Clark enrolled in Harvard's Law School and soon organized a club team. A year later the school was putting its own team on the court with Clark as both coach and captain.

There were no real eligibility rules then, and a player could continue to play as a graduate student, even if he had already participated for four years as an undergrad. But

YMCA teams. Iowa was playing in 1893, Ohio State University by 1894, Temple University in Philadelphia began playing about the same time and a year later the sport found its way to Yale. By 1897 Pennsylvania had joined the hoop parade, as did a number of other schools. It was beginning to look as if basketball at the college level had come to stay.

The first recorded game between two colleges occurred in February 1895, when the Minnesota State School of Agri-

none of that stemmed the growth of the sport. By 1901 a number of Ivy League schools formed an Eastern League, while several schools to the north organized the New England League.

In 1905 the Western Conference (today's Big Ten) was born, as new rivalries were formed and new traditions started. The level of skills was rising rapidly, and the better teams began running up big scores against mismatched opposition. For example, Dartmouth once defeated Boston College by a score of 44-0, and in 1903 Bucknell swamped the Philadelphia College of Pharmacy by the incredible score of 159-5. And equally incredible was the fact that a Bucknell player named John Anderson scored a total of 80 points in the game. That sounds like early Wilt Chamberlain.

There were other unusual performances in the early days. The University of Minnesota, for instance, went unbeaten with a 15-0 record in 1902 and went from there to win 34 straight games through 1904. In 1905 the Columbia team won 26 games in a row and in a post-season tournament defeated both Minnesota and Wisconsin, then proclaimed itself national champion.

Though there wasn't an NCAA Tournament back then, no Final Four to capture the nation's fancy, there were often loosely-held invitational tournaments. In 1904 a national outdoor tourney was held in St Louis and won by Hiram College. But Hiram College as national champs? It was just a matter of bragging rights. There was no real basis for a nationwide champion.

More and more schools began participating in the sport during the first decade of the twentieth century. And like everything else, the rapid growth created some new problems. One was an attempt to provide a permanent governing body for the sport, and another was a problem of increasingly rough play. In some places basketball was beginning to resemble football.

During the very early years it was YMCA officials who basically controlled the game. But as basketball began to grow and spread among the colleges the YMCA gradually lost its dominance. Realising this, Dr Luther Gulick decided that control of the game should pass to the hands of the Amateur Athletic Union (AAU). The problem was that many colleges simply refused to recognize the AAU's authority and wouldn't bend to its directives.

The dispute came to a head during the 1904-05 season, when the AAU suspended Yale for playing a so-called unregistered team. Yale, however, continued to play. And right before its game with Pennsylvania, the AAU informed Penn that if it went ahead with its game against Yale, it too would be subject to suspension.

This didn't sit well with Penn Athletic Director Ralph Morgan. He wasn't about to be blackmailed or bow to that kind of AAU pressure. Instead of cancelling the game, Morgan invited athletic directors and coaches from more than 350 colleges to meet in Philadelphia in April 1905, with the purpose of finding a way for the colleges to get control of their own game.

At first the meeting seemed destined to fail. Representa-

tives of only 15 colleges attended. But Morgan wasn't ready to quit. He formed a committee of seven and scheduled another meeting for the summer. He said he wanted them to try to formulate a set of standardized college rules. And though just four schools were represented at that meeting, a whole lot came out of little.

Coming to New York City in July 1905 were representatives of Penn, Columbia, Princeton and Yale. At a marathon meeting, these men not only wrote out the first set of collegiate basketball rules but also laid the foundation for a meeting the following year that resulted in the formation of the Intercollegiate Athletic Association. While it took time, it was this organization that eventually grew into the huge National Collegiate Athletic Association, still the governing body for college sports today. Though it didn't happen overnight, the groundwork for solving the first problems had been set.

The second crisis had to do with the increasingly rough play in college games. It didn't come at a good time, because in 1909 President Theodore Roosevelt, no shrinking violet, had shown major concern about the growing number of serious injuries in college football. Some said basketball wasn't far behind, and the new Intercollegiate Athletic Association led the fight against this new, brutal image the game had acquired in some circles.

To show just how far it had gone by 1909, the president of Harvard, Dr Charles Eliot, was quoted as saying that "basketball has become even more brutal than football." And there was a story that the captain of the baseball team at

OPPOSITE ABOVE: *The Princeton University team of 1905 had a decidedly modern look. The players appear relaxed and eager to go, though the game was still a very different one back then. With no giants to dominate and dunk, a center jump after each basket and limited shooting skills, the games were almost always very low-scoring.*

ABOVE: *Here is another shot from basketball's early days. The basket is hooked right to the wall and is sewed closed on the bottom. There are no markings on the court, no key or foul line. The entire scene has a rather turn-of-the-century look.*

Yale had stopped one of his players from joining the basketball team because the sport was too rough. Perhaps as the final indictment, Harvard University announced in the spring of 1909 that it was discontinuing basketball, which apparently had been losing popularity at the school. But the official reason, according to one committee member was as follows: "The games more closely resembled free fights than friendly athletic contests between amateur teams."

Sour grapes? Perhaps. You see, Harvard at that time was suffering from an ailment that still causes radical changes at colleges today. It's called a losing program. In any case, the school decided to give up the sport, a decision that would last for some ten years.

LEFT: *Though the early game was a tough one, this team decided to play for laughs when the cameraman appeared. Even the manager was mugging it up. But the thick knee pads show they meant business when the game began.*

BELOW: *Once the game began to spread it went everywhere, even into the high schools. This championship Rhode Island high school quint of 1912-13 shows both pride and comaraderie in their team picture.*

OPPOSITE: *You wouldn't see this ball on a basketball court today. It had a bladder inside and was laced up. But it didn't always keep its shape and give a true bounce or make play any easier.*

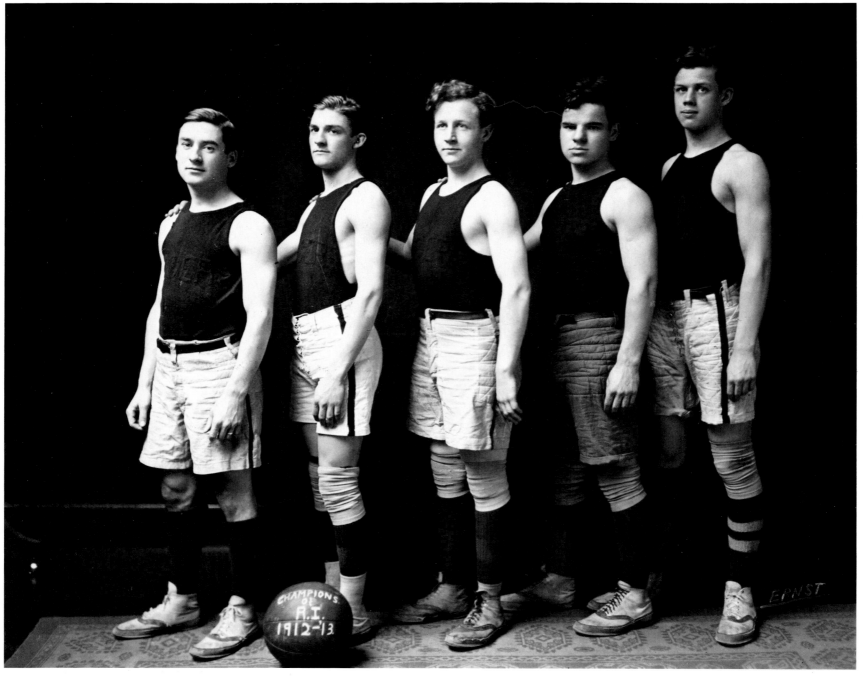

20

But basketball survived. There was really no national effort to abolish the sport and it was more or less allowed to keep its own house in order. Though the Eastern League was disbanded in 1908, it was reformed some two years later. And that same year, 1908, a rule was made that would disqualify a player after he committed five personal fouls in a game. The limit was reduced to four in 1910 and restored to five some time later. A second official was also added in 1910, another step that, it was hoped, would cut down on some of the rough and tumble play that had come under criticism.

Finally, in 1915, the AAU got together with the YMCAs and the International Athletic Association to standardize rules and further stabilize and establish the game as a major sport. And that meeting also signalled the end of the college game's early years, a time of growth and development. Basketball had now become firmly established and would continue to grow and prosper as an intercollegiate sport.

TWO FOR THE PRICE OF ONE

By the war years, 1914 to 1918, there was new evidence of how fast the college game had grown. The evidence was simple: Great teams were appearing in different sections of the country. Yet some schools still played the game outdoors, others in old, outmoded gymnasiums. And as the game increased in popularity, the need for new, bigger and more modern arenas became obvious. Basketball was no longer the baby brother, the new kid on the block.

One of the great early teams was, perhaps surprisingly, the 1913-1917 University of Texas Longhorns. Why surprisingly? Simply because Texas has never been considered a hotbed of basketball, and it wouldn't seem that a sport coming out of the northeast just two decades earlier would be picked up and nearly deified in the Lone Star state. But that's what happened when the Texas cage quintet began winning game after game, beginning with the end of the 1912-1913 season.

The club played its games outdoors then and, like other teams that didn't like to lose, would sometimes blame defeats on the weather. But when the team won its final three games of 1913, it was beginning a 44-game winning streak that would carry right into 1917 and stir the imagination of every Longhorn-loving Texan.

Texas began its streak with a 70-7 shellacking of Southwestern University in 1913, and it ended 45-games later when Rice topped the Longhorns 24-18 in the fifth game of the 1917 season. In between, Texas beat everyone in sight. During 1916 they won all 12 of their games, outscoring their opponents by a margin of 560 points to 185.

The Longhorns had four different coaches during their winning streak, and the names of the star players are largely forgotten now, except maybe by some tall Texans with long memories. Clyde Littlefield was their leading scorer, while Gus "Pig" Dittmar was considered their top defensive player. Pete Edmond was the third member of an outstanding trio that helped extend the length of the streak.

Never before had one college team been so dominant for such a long period of time, and the notoriety the team received had to be a big help to a still-youthful sport. The streak also encouraged the university to build a new indoor gymnasium to accommodate the team. The project began after the 1916 season, but by the time it was finished, many of the top players had been graduated and the team was in decline. But it would be a long time before Littlefield, Dittmar, Edmond and company would be forgotten.

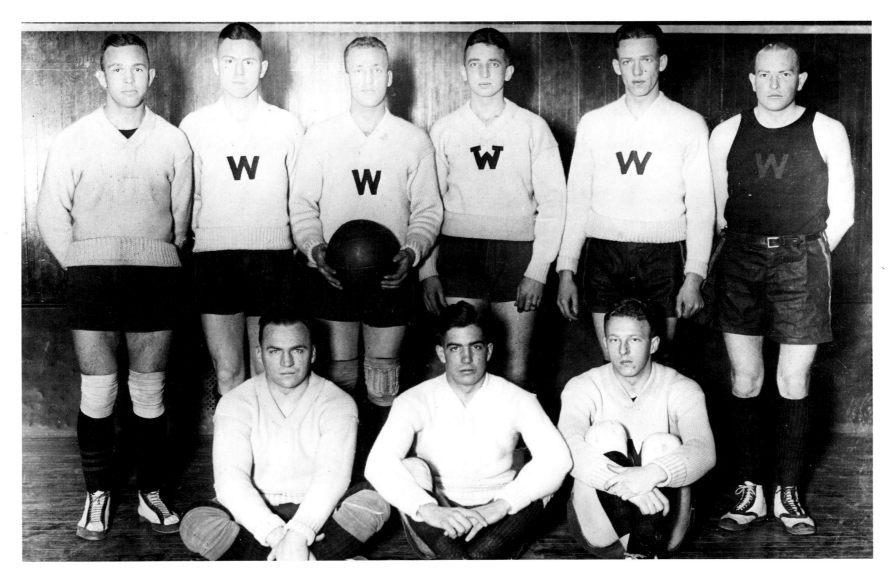

OPPOSITE: *There were some great college teams in the years leading up to and then following World War I. And the sport was being played at the college level from coast to coast. This picture, taken in February of 1918, shows a very serious Yale team in a more traditional basketball pose, even though the Elis were not among the nation's best that year.*

ABOVE: *This is the Wesleyan College basketball team of 1919. Players at the small Connecticut school also took the game very seriously.*

RIGHT: *Members of the 1920 University of Chicago team show how to set a pick.*

During that same period other unbeaten teams included the Universities of Wisconsin (1914), Illinois and Virginia (1915), Oregon State (1918), Navy (1919) and Texas A&M (1920). There were more outstanding teams into the 1920s. Army was unbeaten in 1923, while a year later North Carolina and Texas were also perfect. Montana State was another school that began building a powerful program in the late teens and carried into the 1920s. Ott Romney had a 144-31 coaching record there from 1923 to 1928.

One problem during these years was the lack of cross-sectional play. Most teams played strictly within their own area, and for that reason it was difficult to compare the teams of, say, the South with ballclubs in the East or North. They just never got together on the court.

In addition, there were still a number of rules that continued to hinder the game's overall development. Many contests seemed to be nothing more than a succession of free throws, players walking up and down the court as the referee's whistle sounded again and again. Foul shots were awarded for such things as traveling with the ball and the double dribble. But in 1923 the rules committee changed these breakdowns to violations, meaning only a change of possession, no free throws. That way, the game was faster and could flow much more evenly. And most important, it was better for the spectator.

One rule that stayed in effect until the late 1930s, however, was the center jump after each and every basket. It could be compared to a face-off in hockey, which occurs after a goal. But there were many more scores in basketball, and to stop the game and march everyone back to center court after each hoop really slowed the action and didn't allow teams to fast break after a basket. It hindered the entire game, and it's surprising that the ancient rule lasted as long as it did.

Fortunately, it didn't slow the growth of the game as much as it slowed its pace. Many schools were investing large sums of money in new gymnasiums and field houses specifically built to showcase their basketball teams. Some of them were quite impressive, such as the 16,000-seat facility constructed at the University of Iowa. With more of these new arenas being built during the 1920s, it was as if the colleges were telling everyone that basketball was not only a sport but a money-making proposition as well.

In addition to the local enthusiasms engendered by unbeaten teams in such diverse areas as Texas, Oregon and Wisconsin, basketball was also thriving in the East and in the New York area. In fact, it was in New York City that an event took place in March 1920 that really showed the potential of the college game to turn on the fans and create an atmosphere of basketball mania. There was a natural rivalry in New York between City College and New York University. The two teams met every year, with the rivalry becoming ever more intense. When their 1920 game approached, both teams were in the midst of outstanding seasons. CCNY had a 13-2 record, while NYU was coming in at 11-1. Since NYU didn't have its own gym and had, in fact, played some of its games on a barge in the Hudson River, it was decided to put their game with CCNY into the 168th Street Regimental Armory.

Much to the surprise of many, 10,000 New York City basketball fans crowded into the armory to witness a 39-21 NYU victory. It was perhaps the largest crowd in college basketball history to that time, and a graphic testimony to the drawing power of the court game. NYU and its star player, Howard Cann, went on to win the AAU title in Atlanta later in the year, beating Rutgers for the crown.

With the 1930s approaching quickly, another New York City team came to the fore with an innovative approach to the game that eventually led to several major rule changes. They were the St John's University teams of 1929 to 1931, and they were so good that they earned the collective nickname the Wonder Five. During a three-year period, the Wonder Five won 68 ballgames and lost only four and were dubbed the "smartest college club in the country" by Nat Holman, the City College coach and a professional player. It's no wonder Holman was impressed with the Wonder Five. They used many of the same strategies as the professional Original Celtics, the team that Holman had played for during their heyday in the early 1920s.

To begin with, the Wonder Five had a big center, Matty Begovich. While he was only six feet, two inches, in those days he was considered practically a giant. And because of the center jump after each basket, the Wonder Five had an immediate advantage. The club would then go into a set offense, looking for an open shot. They didn't rush the ball and depended on an outstanding ballhandler, Max Posnack, to control the offense. And if Posnack didn't handle the ball, Mac Kinsbrunner did. He was also a fine dribbler. Rip Gerson and Allie Schuckman rounded out the Wonder Five lineup, and the five men played together for two straight years.

James "Buck" Freeman coached the club and was instrumental in putting in the offense that often drove other teams to distraction. The Wonder Five used a pivot play similar to that of the Original Celtics, with the ball often

ABOVE: *Fordham centers James Delaney, left, and John Gacksyersky leap for the ball during a 1927 practice session at the Fordham gym. The Rams were getting set for an intercity battle against New York University when this picture was taken.*

OPPOSITE ABOVE: *On winning the National AAU title with a win over Rutgers in Atlanta, Georgia, in March 1920, the NYU basketball team was given a hero's welcome in New York.*

RIGHT: *Members of the NYU team proudly display their AAU title trophy.*

going into the pivot man and the others cutting sharply off him to the hoop. They would even occasionally use a double pivot, making it even more difficult for the defenses to cope.

Ironically, the Wonder Five were declared ineligible for further collegiate competition after the 1931 season because it was learned that they had played some extra games against professionals. This didn't bother the players. They simply turned professional themselves, becoming the Brooklyn Jewels and later the New York Jewels, showing the same skills and competitive fires against other pros as they had at St John's.

But before that happened the Wonder Five took part in another piece of basketball history in New York. The date was 21 January 1931, a time of turmoil for many people. The stock market crash had occurred just a little over a year earlier, and the Great Depression was just beginning. With so many New Yorkers out of work, Mayor James J Walker decided to sponsor a tripleheader basketball game at Madison Square Garden to benefit the unemployed.

Because it was a tripleheader, the games were shortened to 15-minute halves, but that didn't dim the enthusiasm of the more than 16,000 fans who attended the extravaganza. In the first game, Columbia defeated Fordham 21-18. Manhattan was next, topping NYU in another close encounter 16-14, and in the third and feature game, the Wonder Five came out and defeated CCNY 17-9. In that game, St John's played such a tight, unyielding defense that after scoring the first basket of the night CCNY did not score another point from the floor until the final minute of the ballgame.

There was one problem, however. One of the largest

crowds ever to see a basketball game — and a crowd that donated some $20,000 for the unemployed — didn't really enjoy the brand of entertainment put forth on that evening long ago. For while they saw three close basketball games, they did not see a great deal of sustained action. And when the Wonder Five went into their deliberate slowdown game the fans began to boo. They did not want to see 17-9 basketball games. That might have been fine in 1900, but this was 1931, and the game should have come farther than this, many reasoned.

What the fans didn't like was the pace. They wanted more action, a faster game with more scoring. Because there was no center line on the court then, a team like St John's often held the ball in its backcourt, or sometimes retreated there when a set play didn't work. The season after, the tripleheader a center line was added to the college game, and the ten-second rule was put into effect. Now the team with the ball had just ten seconds to get it over that halfcourt line and into the offensive zone.

Another change that was already on the horizon was one that would eliminate offensive players standing under the basket to block out defenders near the hoop. In 1935 the three-second rule went into effect, prohibiting offensive players from staying in the lane for more than that allotted amount of time. That also guaranteed more offensive movement and ultimately a more exciting game.

In addition, there were some coaches already envisioning a different kind of basketball. Frank Keaney, for instance, the coach of Rhode Island State College, had an entirely opposite system from St John's in the early 1930s. Keaney's teams used a fast-breaking offense, characterized by long passes and a lot of shooting. His Rhode Island State teams became known as point-a-minute quintets, and their style of play was copied by other teams. If that offense was played today, it might be called run-and-gun, a philosophy still employed by many college teams, such as the University of Nevada at Las Vegas.

So there was more than one way to play the game. That was certainly better than carbon-copy basketball, and with the rule changes designed to speed things up, the game was never in trouble, never really declined in popularity during this period in the early and mid-1930s. In fact, with rivalries becoming ever more intense, the small gymnasiums were often cramped and crowded, with fans being turned away every night.

The famous tripleheader in the Garden in 1931 had been promoted by Dan Daniel, a sportswriter with the *New York World Telegram*. As his assistant he chose a young writer with the paper, Ned Irish, who regularly drew the college basketball beat. Irish knew all about the small, crowded gyms, having once suffering the indignity of tearing his pants while trying to climb through a window into the Manhattan College gym. The capacity of the place was about 500 people, but nearly 1000 spectators had jammed the building, sending Ned Irish through the window in an attempt to get his story.

What a shame, Irish thought, looking around. A game like this should be played in a larger arena. Then he had the germ of an idea. If 16,000 people showed up at the Garden for a tripleheaders, why wouldn't maybe 10,000 show up on a regular basis if someone offered them doubleheaders, two games for the price of one?

OPPOSITE: *The legendary Nat Holman was both a coach and a professional player at the same time. In this 1933 photo he instructs his CCNY team in the art of the underhand free throw.*

RIGHT: *The old Madison Square Garden was the scene of many early college basketball battles still remembered today.*

BELOW: *Edward S "Ned" Irish was the man most responsible for taking the college game out of the small gyms and putting it into major arenas. His first Madison Square Garden double-header in December of 1934 drew more than 16,000 fans and set the stage for the great court extravaganzas of today.*

With the 1934 clash between NYU and CCNY once again on the horizon, Irish made an effort to set up the contest at Madison Square Garden. Alas, there was already a fight card booked for that night, and it was too late to make the change. But Irish didn't give up. He immediately began making plans to do it the following year. This time he asked the Garden to give him six dates for college basketball doubleheaders. He was met with some skepticism from Garden officials and had to make a number of guarantees before the deal was set. Irish was gambling, all right, but he saw the potential in big time college ball and he was determined to follow it up. The job of setting up the first doubleheader was so demanding that Irish quit his job at the *Telegram* and became a fulltime promoter. It was the best decision he ever made.

The first doubleheader was set for 29 December 1934, with St John's against Westminster of Pennsylvania in the first game and NYU playing Notre Dame in the second contest. Westminster had a great center in Wes Bennett, while Notre Dame had a pair of stars in Johnny Jordan and George Ireland. The two New York teams, of course, had huge followings, and all four quintets were in the midst of outstanding seasons. It was a great pair of matchups for the experiment that Ned Irish had gambled so heavily on being successful.

Before the game sportswriter Everett Morris made these comments in his column in the old *New York Herald-Tribune*: "Metropolitan college basketball will step out of its cramped gymnasiums and gloomy armories tonight and into the bright lights and spaciousness of Madison Square Garden for the first of a series of six doubleheaders arranged in the hope of proving this winter that the sport deserves and will thrive in a major league setting."

Thrive it did. With Irish hoping for a crowd of 10,000, some 16,188 fans paid their way into the giant arena to see college basketball. And what they saw was, indeed, great basketball. With Wes Bennett living up to his advance notices with 21 points, Westminster defeated St John's 37-33 in the first game. And in game two Notre Dame came from behind to take a 25-18 victory.

But even more important was the attendance that led to a gate of about $20,000. Ned Irish's gamble had paid off. There wasn't a single complaint from Garden officials, and a week later a second doubleheader took place. This time CCNY topped St John's 32-22 and NYU edged Kentucky 23-22 in a game not decided until the final seconds. The winning point came as a result of a controversial foul call, but despite protesting the call, Kentucky coach Adolph Rupp looked forward to returning with his Wildcats to the Garden. So did other coaches. The large crowds meant more money for the schools, and the New York exposure meant more publicity for the players.

The Garden doubleheaders went a long way toward changing the face of college basketball. In a sense, they were instrumental in bringing the sport right into the modern era. That was still a few years away, but once Ned Irish began doing his thing the sport reached a point where there was no turning back. In the ensuing years, there

OPPOSITE: *Madison Square Garden quickly became the scene of many epic battles between rival New York City schools. This game between City College and St John's was played on 4 January 1936. Number 12, in the dark uniform, battling for the rebound, is the great CCNY star Bernie Fliegel.*

RIGHT: *Out-of-town teams also began flocking to the Garden in the 1930s. In this 1936 battle between New York University and Kentucky, NYU's Irwin Klein shows his wingspan as he gets set to grab a rebound. Almost all the early Garden games were intense battles.*

would be more players and coaches emerging to receive the kind of national recognition that had previously been the personal domain of baseball and football.

New York City continued to be a hotbed of the sport. St John's, City College and NYU had all become major powers in the game already, and in the middle 30s they were joined by still another area school: The LIU Blackbirds began emerging under new coach Clair Bee. The reed-thin Bee, who had overcome tuberculosis as a child, was an innovative coach who surprised the basketball world by directing his Blackbirds to a 26-1 record in 1934. But the Blackbirds played their home games in a hole-in-the-wall gym at the Brooklyn College of Pharmacy, and no one really took them seriously. That is, until they came into the Garden.

In the 1935-36 season the Blackbirds were unbeaten. They had an all-American guard in Julie Bender, who usually controlled the ball. Leo Merson had a great two-hand set shot. The forwards were Ken Kramer and Marius Russo, who would later pitch in the big leagues with the New York Yankees. The center was Art Hillhouse, who was one of the taller men in college ball at the time.

When LIU won its first ten games at the beginning of the 1936-37 season it had built a 43-game winning streak over three seasons and was finally recognized as one of the best teams in the country. Then, on 30 December 1936, the Blackbirds were booked into Madison Square Garden for a game against Stanford University. The game sparked a great deal of interest because it matched a powerhouse team from the East against a powerhouse ballclub from the West. Intersectional play was still rare, and a chance to compare teams separated by 3000 miles and contrasting styles proved an irresistible draw to New York basketball fans.

The East-West meeting was not the only reason area fans flocked to the Garden on that cold December night. Stanford, you see, had a great player who was destined to leave an indelible mark on the game. His name was Hank Luisetti, and he was one of the first players to shoot the ball one-handed. Until Luisetti came along, the two basic shots in college basketball were the driving layup and the two-handed set shot, taken with both feet planted on the court.

Angelo "Hank" Luisetti, a native of San Francisco, first learned his innovative way of shooting at Galileo High

School, where coach Tommy DeNike showed it to some of his players. "A number of my players would use the shot in practice," DeNike once said, "but they would only use it in a game once in a while. Hank was different. He wasn't afraid to take the shot in a game. And while the others used it, nobody took it quite like Hank."

Luisetti grew to a lanky six feet, two inches and was more than just a fine shooter. He had court presence, was a leader, a fine ballhandler who sometimes used a behind-the-back dribble and a tenacious defensive player. In other words, he played a complete game, though it was the one-handed shot that got him the most publicity.

There were still many coaches who wouldn't tolerate one-handed shooting, but when Luisetti came to Stanford he asked the coach there, John Burn, if he could continue shooting his way. Once the coach saw how quickly Luisetti got the shot off, and also saw its accuracy, he gave the youngster his blessing. There was no way any coach in his right mind would try to change a player like Hank Luisetti. He could take his one-hander standing flat-footed, or he could launch off the dribble, making it look like a running jump shot.

And from the opening tap against LIU, before some 18,000 fans at Madison Square Garden, Hank Luisetti showed everyone that he was for real. He was the dominant figure at both ends of the court. His running one-handers electrified the huge crowd, but at the other end he was right in there too, working on defense and rebounding under the hoop.

Behind the play of Luisetti, Stanford jumped off to an early lead that the Indians never lost. They defeated the Blackbirds easily, 45-31, as Luisetti scored 15 points. When he was removed from the game with less than a minute remaining he received a huge standing ovation from the New York crowd. This was the kind of thrilling basketball action they had paid to see.

Hank Luisetti would go on to set a four-season national scoring record with 1596 points. And in a game played on 1 January 1938 he astounded the basketball world by scoring 50 points against Duquesne: Of course, the abolition of the center jump by then helped make the record possible. While he never played pro ball, opting for a business career and

LEFT: *Posing for the camera is the 1936 Stanford team that featured the great Angelo "Hank" Luisetti, perhaps the greatest scorer of his time and early proponent of the one-handed shot. Left to right, Arthur Stoefen, Luisetti, Howard Turner, Capt Dinty Moore, and Jack Caldewood.*

OPPOSITE: *Clair Bee's LIU team had won 43 straight games when it met Stanford at the Garden on 30 December 1936. But it was Luisetti, with 15 points and a great floor game, that derailed the Blackbirds 45-31. In this photo, LIU's great Art Hillhouse goes high after his own rebound in what would be a losing cause.*

some AAU action, Hank Luisetti was one of a kind, a very great college player who helped shape the future of his sport.

What Hank Luisetti showed New York and all of college basketball was the future. His style of play was crowd-pleasing in itself, and with another couple of restrictions removed, many felt the game would have even greater potential as a nationwide attraction. In addition, the increase in sectional play and the willingness of teams to travel across the country got some people to thinking about post-season tournaments. That would be a way to get some of the best teams from all over the country together, maybe even a way to determine a national champion.

There was one rule, many felt, that was still keeping the game from really opening up, and that was the necessity of the center jump after every basket. Those who wanted the rule to stay argued that the fast pace of the game would be too much for the players if they didn't get that brief rest that came when they would set up the center jump. Without it, a team could put the ball in play under the defensive hoop immediately after a basket was scored.

But there was another consideration. Because the clock continued to run during the repeated center jumps, it was estimated that the elimination of the practice would add some nine to 12 minutes of play to each game. You would be giving the fans a much more action-packed and complete package. So prior to the 1937-38 season the deed was done. The center jump after each basket had become a piece of basketball history, a trivia question for future generations.

The difference was evident immediately. At the outset of the 1937-38 season the scores were markedly higher and

there was an increased emphasis on the offensive part of the game. In fact, the first doubleheader of the year saw St John's and Illinois set a Garden scoring record, as the Illini won the game 60-45. The effect of the rule change was thus immediately obvious, and the fans loved it. And that spurred Ned Irish and others to set the wheels in motion for another big change, a post-season tournament to be held at their showcase arena, Madison Square Garden.

During the winter of 1938 plans were formulated to hold the tourney right after the regular season ended. The Metropolitan Basketball Writers Association was the official sponsor of the event, and it would be named the National Invitation Tournament. The organizers looked for an East-West flavor for the first time, and the six teams chosen were NYU, LIU, Temple, Bradley, Oklahoma A&M and Colorado. Temple, with a 23-2 record during the regular season, was installed as the favorite, and the Owls didn't disappoint their fans.

In opening night play NYU defeated city rival LIU 39-37, while Temple rolled over Bradley 53-40. Then, in the semifinals, Colorado squeaked past NYU 48-47, while Temple topped Hank Iba's Oklahoma A&M team 54-44. One of the stars of the Colorado team, incidentally, was Byron "Whizzer" White, who was also a football all-American and who would later become a justice of the United States Supreme Court.

Playing before a packed Garden house in the finals, Temple showed it had a great team in 1938 by easily topping Colorado 60-36 to take the first NIT crown and, in the eyes of many, become the national champions. The tournament had been such a resounding success that the National Colle-

giate Athletic Association decided to hold a national tournament of its own, beginning with the following season.

Now there would be a pair of post-season events to stir the imagination of college basketball fans everywhere. With the NIT and NCAA tourneys every year, East could meet West, North could meet South on neutral ground, and any doubts as to which teams played the best brand of basketball could be dispelled. The game had taken another quantum leap, with a great deal of the credit belonging to Ned Irish. For it was Irish who had best understood what was really needed to make basketball an important spectator sport. It was Irish who saw the college game as one that should be in large arenas, offering fans two for the price of one.

OPPOSITE BELOW: *Colorado, with future Supreme Court Justice Byron "Whizzer" White, gets ready to meet NYU in the semi-finals of the very first National Invitation Tournament in 1938. Left to right are Dick Harvey, "Swisher" Schwartz, White, Jim Willcoxen, and Don Hendricks. Colorado won*

BELOW: *Teams from the Midwest also began coming into the Garden, often to the dismay of locals. In this December 1937 contest Gerry Bush (4) of St John's is pushed off a rebound during Illinois' 60-45 win.*

LAND OF THE GIANTS

In a sense, the 1938-39 season represented the beginning of a new era in college basketball. It was the first year of the NCAA Tournament, an event that would grow into one of the major sports spectacles in America. But that first year it was decided that there would be only an eight-team field.

The teams would be picked by selection committees from each of the eight regions represented, with one team from each region. In those early years the pattern that developed saw the NCAA take mostly teams that were affiliated with a conference, while the NIT took the independent teams. That made for two interesting tournaments, each with its share of outstanding ballclubs. Both tourneys had equally strong fields, and it stayed that way for many years before the NCAA was finally recognized as the event which decided the national championship.

Perhaps the best team of the 1938-39 season was again Long Island University. Clair Bee had put together another powerful ballclub, one that finished the regular season unbeaten. The Blackbirds had solid senior starters in all-America Irv Torgoff, Danny Kaplowitz, Dolly King, George Newman and Mike Sewitch. But Coach Bee also had three sensational sophomores – Ossie Shechtman, Solly Schwartz and Cy Lobello – to give the Long Island team truly outstanding depth.

LEFT: *Long Island coach Clair Bee in a 1949 photo. Bee coached the Blackbirds for 18 seasons, in which he won 327 games and lost just 67.*

ABOVE: *Irv Torgoff was the star of Bee's 1939 LIU team that went unbeaten and then won the NIT championship.*

OPPOSITE ABOVE: *The great LIU team of 1938-39. Left to right, Dan Kaplowitz, George Newman, Art Hillhouse, Irv Torgoff and John Bromberg.*

OPPOSITE RIGHT: *Dan Kaplowitz of LIU fires one up in a game against Southern California. The Blackbirds beat the West Coast team 33-18.*

The Blackbirds were unbeaten going into the season finale with LaSalle in Philadelphia's Convention Hall. LaSalle played a slowdown game in an attempt to steal a victory, and they held a slim lead for much of the night. Coach Bee had his team hang loose, biding its time. Finally, late in the game, Johnny Bromberg of LIU stepped to the foul line with a chance to give the Blackbirds the lead. Suddenly, and without warning, a LaSalle player walked over to Bromberg and punched him in the nose.

What followed was a minor riot, with many fans charging out of the stands to attack the LIU players. When order was finally restored LIU went on to complete a 28-21 victory, but Bromberg's nose had been broken and Mike Sewitch had suffered a broken arm. It was an ugly incident and a tough way for the Blackbirds to complete their second unbeaten season in four years.

But the victory also made them favorites in the NIT tournament, where they figured their toughest opposition would be unbeaten Loyola of Chicago. The NCAA tourney didn't have the luxury of an undefeated team, Oregon having perhaps the best mark at 26-5. The NIT field was probably a bit stronger.

Sure enough, in the finals it was LIU against Loyola. Clair Bee knew his team would have to contend with the shotblocking abilities of six-foot, eight-inch Mike Novak, and he had shooters like Torgoff and Kaplowitz practice banking shots high off the backboard. Defensively, Bee had the six-foot, four-inch Sewitch play Novak, despite the fact that Sewitch's arm, broken in the LaSalle game, was still in a cast. Yet the burly Sewitch was able to force Novak outside, and that may have been the turning point of the game. LIU won it 44-32, a game Clair Bee would call his greatest victory.

LEFT: *More and more big basketball battles took place at the Garden into the 1940s. In February of 1940 action, Robert Sherry of Fordham (dark jersey) battles Pitt's Sol Levin for a rebound in a game won by the Panthers 57-37.*

The NCAA finals that year pitted Oregon against Ohio State. The Buckeyes were just 14-6 in the regular season, but played well in the tournament, coming on to defeat Villanova in the semi-finals 53-36, with Jim Hull scoring 28 points. Oregon won its way into the semis, where they put it to Oklahoma 55-37. The final game was played at the Patton Gym on the Northwestern University campus in Evanston, Illinois on 27 March.

Oregon was considered a very big team for its day. The Ducks had six-foot, eight-inch Slim Wintermute at center and a pair of six-foot, four-inch forwards, Laddie Gale and John Dick. They were nicknamed "The Tall Firs". Yet in the final game it was five-foot, eight Bobby Anet who did as much damage as any of the Tall Firs. With Anet handling the ball expertly, the Ducks led by a 21-16 count at the half and then pulled away for a 46-33 victory, becoming college basketball's first ever NCAA champion. John Dick finished with 15 points, while Anet had ten. Jim Hull led Ohio State with 15.

Shortly after the beginning of the 1939-40 season an era sadly came to an end. On 28 November the basketball world learned of the death of Dr James Naismith. Naismith must have been pleased with the game he created. He had seen it spread nationwide, evolving from a recreational activity to a major sport that was continuing to grow in popularity.

There was another milestone event during the same season. It happened on 28 February 1940, when an experimental television station, W2XBS, and a forerunner of WNBC in New York, televised basketball for the first time. The station aired a Madison Square Garden doubleheader in which Pittsburgh played Fordham and NYU met Georgetown. Though the picture was lost for a portion of both games, the TV experiment was a foreshadowing of where the game was going and what its future held.

Colorado won the NIT title that year, downing Duquesne 51-40, and Indiana won its first NCAA crowd with an easy 60-42 victory over Kansas. But in the eyes of many, the best team in the country didn't play in either tournament, for the Seton Hall Pirates, under coach John "Honey" Russell, had won all their 19 regular season games.

Seton Hall was led by a guard named Bob Davies, a slick all-around performer who electrified the crowds with his ballhandling and outstanding defensive play. Davies had read about Hank Luisetti's behind-the-back dribble and made it an integral part of his own game. He was a court showman at a time when that kind of play was often frowned upon. "I've always been grateful for Honey Russell letting me play the kind of game I wanted to play," Davies would say in later years. "I was starting to throw a lot of behind-the-back passes and dribbling behind my back. I didn't go out there with the intention of being fancy. It was just different ways to try to get the ball to someone. If you had to throw it behind your head or around your back, or some other way, you did it."

Seton Hall was unbeaten again the next year, and this time they were invited to the NIT. But in the semi-finals that year the Pirates ran into another strong LIU team, and Clair Bee's charges defeated Seton Hall 49-26, with Solly Schwartz doing a defensive job on Davies. LIU then went on to defeat Ohio University 56-42 and win the championship.

Wisconsin came out of nowhere to win the NCAA title with a victory over Washington State in the finals, 39-34, with all-American center Gene Englund the big star. The game also marked the end of basketball's first 50 years, if 1891 is used as the starting date. And while the game had made great strides in a relatively short time, there were more major changes coming.

Basketball continued during the war years, for sports were a welcome diversion during the early 1940s, taking people's minds off the war effort and worry about loved ones overseas. Stanford became the 1942 NCAA champion, beating Dartmouth, while West Virginia topped an Adolph Rupp Kentucky team 47-45 to cop the NIT crown. But by the next season, 1942-43, the war began to strip many of the colleges of their best players. To compensate, freshmen were declared eligible for the first time so that college teams could continue to compete. A few schools, however, did drop their programs temporarily. In addition, wartime restrictions on travel cut down on the number of intersectional games. Teams stayed close to home and on many occasions replaced cancelled games against other schools with YMCA and AAU teams.

Yet despite the effects of the war, there was never any thought of cancelling an entire season. Basketball was too important a tonic for an increasingly war-weary nation. And strangely enough, this was the year in which the arrival of two new players would change the face of the court game forever. Perhaps it was simply coincidence, or maybe just a natural evolution that would have overtaken the game sooner or later, but in 1942-43, these two men began their college careers amidst the sneers of skeptics that they would never be able to really play the game. The reason: They were too tall!

A bespectacled, six-foot, ten-inch freshman named George Mikan was starting his career at De Paul University in Chicago, while another gangling frosh, seven-foot Bob Kurland, had entered Oklahoma A&M. Kurland was nicknamed "Foothills" because his feet tangled so often as he ran up and down the court, while Mikan was so nearsighted that he had to wear his glasses even during games.

Sure, there had been an occasional giant in the sport, but none of them had ever demonstrated much agility or innate skill. And more often than not, people looked upon them as freaks rather than athletes. In fact, Mikan worked out at

LEFT: *Bob Davies of Seton Hall was one of the exciting college players of the 1940s. One of the first to use the behind-the-back dribble, Davies often brought the crowd to its feet with his passing wizardry. He later went on to an equally great pro career and is in the Basketball Hall of Fame.*

OPPOSITE: *Big George Mikan (left), shown with his brother, Eddie, was one of basketball's first great big men. The 6-10 Mikan was to prove that a giant could also be an outstanding hoop player. He was a star at DePaul University in the 1940s and then with the pro Minneapolis Lakers on into the 1950s.*

Notre Dame shortly after enrolling at De Paul and was politely told by the coach there, George Keogan, to go back to De Paul because "you'll make a better scholar than a basketball player."

Giants like Mikan and Kurland needed a lot of work for the simple reason that they hadn't started playing the game early enough. Basketball is not a sport that can be picked up overnight, especially by a big man. As Mikan was to say in later years: "No matter where a tall guy went in those days there was always someone to tell him he couldn't do something. So it took a great deal of determination for me to prove I could do anything anyone else could do."

Under Ray Meyer at De Paul, Mikan began working hard at all the fundamentals of the game. And because of his great size, he started with basic coordination, never even touching a basketball for about a month. "Coach Meyer had me jumping rope, doing a lot of figure eights, running around chairs, lifting weights, boxing, dancing, running with the track team, all kinds of things like that. I also did a lot of hand and eye coordination work and a lot of work on my legs. . . ."

Like many of players of the day, George Mikan was pri-

marily a right handed shooter. But Ray Meyer wanted him to be a complete player, to be able to shoot with either hand, and he worked with him constantly to develop his left hand. By the time he was a junior, Mikan could shoot either way.

It was a similar learning experience for Bob Kurland at Oklahoma A&M under Hank Iba. Kurland had come to college strictly for the purpose of getting his education and even after joining the basketball team found himself labelled as a "glandular goon" by one rival coach. But he did many of the same things Mikan did, such as jumping rope and working on his movement. "I never had the type of strength Mikan had," Kurland was to say, "so I never developed the same kind of inside game with the sweeping hook shot. Rather, I learned how to work a defender into position and take a quick little jump-push shot."

The development of Mikan and Kurland and a few other big men of the time, such as six-foot, nine-inch Harry Boykoff of St John's, eventually changed the face and pace of the game. While more and more schools were going to a quick, fast-breaking offense, Iba at Oklahoma A&M was able to stay with a slow, deliberate attack. The reason was Bob Kurland. "Kurland made our type of game go," the

LEFT: *George Mikan (99) towers over his opponents to grab a rebound as DePaul meets Indiana State in a 1945 game. Mikan not only had size and strength, but had the determination to become a great player and remain one. Many think he would still be outstanding if he played today.*

OPPOSITE: *Mikan's biggest rival was seven-foot Bob 'Foothills' Kurland of Oklahoma A & M. Kurland did not have Mikan's strength, but worked hard to become a great all-American. Here the two giants meet during the 1944 NIT Tourney in New York. DePaul won the game 41-38. Instead of playing in the NBA like Mikan, Kurland went on to play AAU ball for the Phillips 66ers.*

coach said. "We knew he was there to get us the ball, so we never had to rush into a bad shot."

But perhaps the biggest change was on defense. When Mikan and Kurland arrived on the scene, defensive players were still allowed to knock the ball away anytime before it reached the hoop. But the new big men became so adept at this that by 1945 the goaltending rule went into effect. It prohibited a player from knocking the ball away once it started its downward trajectory toward the basket. It's the same rule that is still in effect today.

As freshmen, neither Mikan nor Kurland was yet a superstar. Mikan was a little further advanced. He averaged 11 points a game, and De Paul made it to the NCAA tournament, only to lose in the second round to the eventual finalist, Georgetown, 53-49. Kurland averaged just 2.5 points a game in the 1942-43 season, so the jury on him was still out. But Hank Iba was working him incessantly. "I wanted Bob to develop a little left-handed hook," Iba recalled. "The first day he tried it he took about 600 shots. The first 100 or so didn't hit anything, the backboard or the rim. The next 100 didn't go in, either. But after that he began connecting."

Wyoming, behind Kenny Sailors' 16 points, won the NCAA title in 1943, defeating Georgetown in the finals, while St John's and Harry Boykoff won the NIT easily,

defeating Toledo. But by the next season the two big men, Mikan and Kurland, began to dominate the game and would continue doing so for the next three years, each making first team all-American for the remainder of their college careers.

Of course the war continued to affect the game, and at the beginning of the 1943-44 season De Paul almost didn't field a team. But the Blue Demons were able to round up a squad and by the end of the season were invited to the NIT Tournament. Also in that field was Iba's Oklahoma A&M team. So there was a chance that Mikan and Kurland would be meeting each other for the first time.

A 68-45 De Paul victory over Muhlenberg, coupled with Oklahoma A&M's 43-29 win over Canisius, set up the confrontation of the giants before a packed house at Madison Square Garden. Although De Paul eventually won the game 41-38, the battle in the middle was something of a standoff. Big George fouled out early in the second half after scoring just nine points. Kurland tallied 14, but his club still lost. De Paul may have peaked too soon, for in the finals the Blue Demons were beaten by a young St John's team 47-39, as Mikan had a sluggish 13 points. Kurland and his club also lost, Kentucky topping them in the consolation game 45-29. With the two big men getting most of the publicity, St John's freshman Billy Kotsores took the MVP prize.

There was still another irony in 1944 postseason play. Utah had gone to the NIT after turning down an NCAA bid, the reason being that only two of the Utah players had ever been to New York, and they preferred going to the Big Apple rather than Kansas City, where the NCAA Tournament was being held. When they were beaten in the first round, they were ready to pack it in and head home.

But suddenly they heard some distressing news. Several members of the NCAA-bound Arkansas team were in a bad car accident, bad enough to knock them out of the tourney. With just two days before the opening of play, the NCAA needed another team and gave Utah a second chance. This time the Utes accepted, hoping to make up for their NIT defeat.

"We went into the NCAA Tournament without practicing and without a scouting report on the other teams," recalled Arnie Ferrin, who was the freshman star of the team. "We just went out there and played." Play they did. First the Utes defeated Missouri 45-35. Next, they won the West championship with a 40-31 victory over Iowa State. Suddenly this Cinderella team was in the finals against Eastern champion Dartmouth. Once again Utah headed for New York, as the title game was set for the Garden.

It turned out to be one of the most exciting finals to that time. Led by Ferrin and the five-foot, seven-inch Wat Misaka, the Utes stayed with Dartmouth all the way. Going into the final seconds, Utah had a 36-34 lead and seemed to have the title wrapped up. But Dartmouth's Dick McGuire

then electrified the crowd with a desperation, halfcourt heave that went in to tie the game.

In the overtime, Ferrin converted on four free throws, but it was Herb Wilkinson's one-hander from the top of the key in the closing seconds that gave Utah a 42-40 victory and the championship. Ferrin was the tourney's MVP, and a week later he led his club against NIT winner St John's in a special Red Cross benefit game. A record crowd of 15,000 had witnessed the title game, and now some 18,000 New Yorkers crammed the Garden for the Red Cross contest. Utah won that one too, by a 43-36 count, making up for their NIT defeat and capping a Cinderella story that even today would be difficult to match.

The next two years belonged to Mikan and Kurland, years in which they showed the basketball world just what a big man could do. For starters, the 1944-45 season was the first with the new goaltending rule in effect. To many, it was a rule made to legislate against the two giants, with the powers that be figuring the effectiveness of both would be limited if they could no longer reach up and swat shots away as the ball descended toward the basket. And it would also be a lesson to all big men to follow: Basketball wouldn't be a cakewalk for them.

But it was their opponents who wouldn't have the cakewalk, for both Mikan and Kurland were just as effective after the goaltending rule as before. Maybe even more effective, because they were both a year older, a year more experienced and had another 12 months to mature as ball-

players. With many teams still hurting due to the war, De Paul and Oklahoma A&M continued to garner the headlines. Mikan led the nation in scoring, but because their NCAA choice from the Midwest usually came from the Big Ten, De Paul went to the NIT. Meanwhile, Kurland led Hank Iba's Aggies into the NCAA championships.

It was in the NIT that Mikan showed the basketball world just how dominant a player he had become. In the opening round De Paul easily defeated West Virgina 76-52, as big number 99 exploded for 33 points. To those who had not seen De Paul before, the victory still had to be something of a surprise. Mikan was big, all right, but not particularly fast, and still had a scholarly appearance with his glasses. In fact, four of the five De Paul starters wore glasses, making them look more like an all-academic team. And one of the starters was just 16 years old. But on the court they *were* a team. Ray Meyer had them working together and playing to their strength, which was Mikan.

OPPOSITE: *Freshman star Arnie Ferrin of Utah (with ball) passing to teammate Wat Misaka (21) en route to leading the Utes to the NCAA title in 1944. Ferrin had 22 points in his final college game before entering the service.*

RIGHT: *It's Mikan again, this time scoring against LIU in a 1945 game.*

BELOW: *Wat Misaka (21) and Bob Lewis (31) of Utah outrace St John's Wade Duym (14) during the 1944 Red Cross championship game.*

In the semi-finals against Rhode Island State, De Paul looked like a team with a mission. And so did Mikan. State's coach, Frank Keaney, made the mistake of predicting in the press that his team would "drive Mikan nuts" with a fast-break attack that would have the big man "stumbling over his own feet." Keaney said that Mikan would go back to Chicago "with his tongue hanging out before we're through with him."

Coach Meyer didn't have a difficult job giving his team a pep talk before the game. He simply repeated Keaney's words, and the Blue Demons went out and played like a team possessed. They attacked Rhode Island State all night, and Mikan was just superb, playing both ends of the court. When it ended, De Paul had a 97-53 victory, and George Mikan's point total equalled that of the entire Rhode Island State team. That's right, the big guy electrified the Garden crowd with a 53-point performance.

The final against Bowling Green was almost anti-climactic. But Mikan had still another challenge, since the Falcons had a young six-foot, 11-inch center named Don Otten. Despite trailing by an 11-0 count after the first five minutes, De Paul rallied behind Mikan to win the championship 71-54, as big George popped for 34 additional points and an unanimous MVP award.

Now basketball fans eagerly awaited the outcome of the NCAA championships, for the annual Red Cross charity game was still in effect, and if Oklahoma A&M could take that title, it would set up a confrontation between Mikan and Kurland. The Aggies didn't disappoint. In the first round they defeated a Utah team that had lost Arnie Ferrin and Fred Sheffield to military service by a 62-37 count, with Kurland contributing 28 points. From there they easily whipped Arkansas 68-41 and entered the finals against New York University. NYU featured an all-American in Sid

OPPOSITE LEFT: *Making it look easy, Mikan scores a Madison Square Garden record 53rd point in a March 1945, game against Rhode Island State. DePaul won the game 97-53, setting still another Garden mark. The 6-10 Mikan broke the old Garden record of 45 points that had been set by Harry Boykoff of St John's.*

OPPOSITE CENTER: *Mikan didn't only play against little guys. In the 1945 NIT final he went up against 6-11 Don Otten of Bowling Green. Though Otten is shown hitting a basket here, Mikan outscored him 34-7, and DePaul won the game 71-54.*

LEFT: *In three NIT games in 1945 George Mikan scored 120 points, an average of 40 a game, almost unheard of in the 1940s. It was hardly a surprise to anyone when the big guy walked off with the Most Valuable Player award.*

Tannenbaum and a skinny six-foot, eight-inch freshman center named Dolph Schayes, who would go on to a great career in the NBA.

With a capacity Garden crowd urging them on, the Violets played the Aggies tough. But Coach Iba's slowdown game stiffled the NYU fast break and held the normally high-scoring Tannenbaum to just four points. Kurland, in the meantime, scored 22 and played his usual fine defensive game, as the Aggies prevailed 49-45 to win the title. Kurland was the MVP, and now the dream matchup with De Paul would become a reality.

But as with many events of great anticipation, this one was something of a disappointment. Both big men were hampered by foul trouble. In fact, Mikan fouled out after just 14 minutes were gone in the first half. He wound up with just nine points. Kurland didn't do much better, scoring only 14, but the Aggies hung on for a 52-44 victory.

With the war destined to end in just a few months, it would be the last Red Cross game ever, but Bob Kurland would still call it "the game" of his college career.

The following year many of the players began returning from service, some joining their old teams for a final hurrah. But it was still Mikan and Kurland who got most of the headlines. In fact, with teams again at full strength, the two big men showed once and for all that they could dominate their sport against any and all competition. Mikan and De Paul were 19-5 for the year, with the big guy again leading the country in scoring with a 23-point average. The Blue Demons, however, did not appear in postseason play in 1946.

Kurland and the Aggies were 28-2 in the regular season, and while Foothills averaged 19 points a game in Iba's deliberate style, he showed everyone what he could do in the final game of the year against St Louis University. Coach

LEFT: *After graduating from Oklahoma A & M, big Bob Kurland said no to the pros. Instead, he took a job with the Phillips Petroleum Corp and joined their AAU team, the Phillips 66ers. Kurland remained a star for years. He played on a pair of Olympic teams, and he also became an executive with the corporation.*

BELOW: *When he was playing for Hank Iba at Oklahoma A & M, Bob Kurland was a basketball giant in many ways. Here he goes up for two points in a March 1946 game against Kansas that the Aggies won 49-38. During his college career Kurland led the Aggies to a pair of NCAA titles.*

Iba decided to let his team loosen up, and the rest of the Aggies kept feeding the ball to Kurland, who exploded for a whopping 58 points. Coming off that, the Aggies defeated Baylor and California en route to the NCAA finals against North Carolina, led by their rail-thin six-foot, six center, Bones McKinney. It turned out to be a tight one. McKinney did a nice job staying with Kurland, but finally fouled out in the second half. Minutes later, the big guy also fouled out of the game. But his teammates hung on without him to win it 43-40, giving the Aggies a second straight NCAA title.

Mikan of course went on to an equally successful pro career, leading the Minneapolis Lakers to a number of NBA championships. Bob Kurland, however, went another route. He began a business career with the Phillips Petroleum Corporation and played many years for the Phillips 66ers in amateur AAU competition. He also found time to play for a pair of gold medal-winning Olympic teams.

George Mikan and Bob Kurland — they came on the scene together and in four years showed basketball its future. They were both instrumental in directing the sport toward the land of the giants, where it still resides.

POSTWAR TRIUMPH AND TRAGEDY

With the graduation of both Mikan and Kurland many returning college players breathed a sigh of relief as the 1946-47 season got underway. No longer would they have to face the two behemoths again . . . unless they met in future years in the NBA or the AAU. But even before the previous season ended it was obvious that new stars were coming on to take over the leadership of the sport.

Kentucky had won the NIT title in 1946, led by a slick freshman guard named Ralph Beard. He would be joined the following year by a six-foot, seven-inch center, Alex Groza, to form the nucleus of perhaps Adolph Rupp's greatest Kentucky team ever. Rhode Island's Ernie Calverly had been the MVP of the NIT, even though Kentucky won, and 17-year-old Ernie Vandeweghe of Colgate was the MVP in an East-West all-star game at the end of the season. Arnie

Ferrin was back at Utah after his stint in the military, and Holy Cross had a star in George Kafton, as well as a young freshman guard named Bob Cousy, who would eventually have his own impact on both the college and pro games. And Dolph Schayes was back at NYU, a year older and a year better.

So college basketball was still in good hands, despite the loss of the supergiants, Mikan and Kurland. And the 1946-47 season was a successful one. Holy Cross, the little Massachusetts school without a gymnasium to call its own, wrote the big story of the year. Under veteran coach Alvin "Doggie" Julian the Crusaders were a mediocre 4-3 after their first seven games. But suddenly the team caught fire, and under the cool court generalship of six-foot, three-inch George Kafton the club won its final 20 games in succes-

OPPOSITE ABOVE: *An NCAA title is the ultimate for every college coach. Here Doggie Julian and his 1947 Holy Cross team pick up the hardware after their win.*

ABOVE: *Bob Cousy of Holy Cross and Kentucky's Ken Rollins (26) go after a loose ball in the 1948 NCAA tourney. The Wildcats won the game 60-52.*

RIGHT: *A long shot of the 1947 Holy Cross-Oklahoma game played in Madison Square Garden on 25 March. Holy Cross' 58-47 victory made it the first eastern team to win the tourney.*

early-season loss to St Louis that led to Rupp changing his game plan somewhat and concentrating more on working the ball inside to Groza, who had become a dominant inside player. After that the Wildcats rolled.

Rupp apparently wanted his club to be the first to win both the NIT and NCAA tournaments in the same year, and the Wildcats were favored to do it. But in the opening round of the NIT they came a cropper against Loyola of Chicago, losing a 61-56 shocker. It would be a game that would come back to haunt the Wildcats, especially Groza and Beard, in the ensuing years.

But there was still the NCAAs, and the Wildcats reverted to their fastbreaking, high-scoring selves, topping Villanova 85-72. They then whipped Illinois with no trouble 76-47 and entered the finals against another Hank Iba Oklahoma State team. But Iba didn't have a Bob Kurland this time, and while the Wildcats were tired from a cross-country train ride from New York to the finals in Seattle, they promptly won their second straight NCAA title 46-36 behind MVP Groza's 25 points. It was trophy time once again.

Groza, Beard and Jones were all named first team all-Americans that year, and in an unprecedented move, the three were allowed to stay together to form the nucleus of a new NBA team, the Indianapolis Olympians. It looked as if they would move immediately into successful and lucrative pro careers, riding in on their collegiate reputations and their immense talents. But for Groza and Beard, as well as a host of other collegians and the game itself, tragedy was just around the corner.

ABOVE: *Coach Nat Holman maps out basketball strategy for one of his fine City College teams of the late 1940s and early 1950s.*

OPPOSITE ABOVE: *CCNY's Irwin Dambrot (5) flies through the air.*

RIGHT: *A happy Loyola team hoists center Jack Kerris after the 1949 win.*

Meanwhile, the college game would have one more glorious season, a season in which Nat Holman's City College team would accomplish what Rupp and the Wildcats tried but failed to do the year before, capture both the NIT and NCAA titles in a single year.

Nat Holman was still a big name in basketball circles. He had been a great professional player with the Original Celtics in the early days of the pro game and had doubled as City College coach since 1920, when he was still in his prime as a player. City College was not like most other schools. There was no tuition, and the academic standards were very high. Understandably, most of New York City's top players went elsewhere. That left Holman to search the Big Apple for whatever talent might be left.

For years, Holman taught a highly-disciplined, short-passing game similar to that played by his pro team. But college ball was changing, and the style of the Original Celtics didn't fit anymore. Reluctant to change his ways, Holman suffered through a number of losing seasons before seeing the error of his ways. After World War II ended, Nat Holman decided to catch up with the times, allowing his players to shoot one-handed and run the fast break.

CCNY had a senior starter in six-foot, four-inch Irwin Dambrot, and he was joined by four sophomores, giving the Beavers a young team that Holman expected to win big for three more years. Ed Warner was a six-foot, two-and-a-half forward and a talented player. At center was six-foot, six Ed Roman, while Al Roth and Floyd Layne started at guard. Both were six-foot, three, a very tall backcourt combination for that time.

The team won 13 of its first 15 games that year and appeared to be headed for a super season. But in its final seven games the club slumped and won only four of them, giving CCNY a 17-5 slate for the year. It was good, but to Nat Holman, always a perfectionist, it wasn't good enough. The veteran coach didn't even think his ballclub would get a tournament bid. The NIT had a 12-team field then, and for some reason the selection committee was having trouble filling the spots. Finally, with one opening remaining, the committee looked homeward and tapped CCNY to fill the slot.

In the first round, City College had to meet defending champion San Francisco. The Dons were heavy favorites, but Holman surprised them by using the same kind of slow-down game they liked to play. Ed Warner scored 26 points, and the Beavers won 65-46.

Next was Kentucky, and Adolph Rupp had a young seven-footer named Bill Spivey in the lineup. The lanky sophomore was averaging about 20 points a game and had led the Wildcats to a 25-4 mark in regular season play. This time Holman had his club running again, and CCNY's fast-break offense and crisp passing proved too much for the

Wildcats. Spivey and the rest of his teammates just couldn't keep up with the New York club, and the Beavers' 89-50 victory turned into one of the worst beatings in Kentucky basketball history. Warner had 26 for the second straight game, while Dambrot chipped in with 20 and Roman wound up with 17.

A 62-52 upset of Duquesne put CCNY in the finals, where they would be meeting the Bradley Braves. Bradley had a solid team and a pair of all-Americans, Paul Unruh and Gene "Squeaky" Melchiorre. Coach Holman had been ill with a high fever, and for a while it looked as if he would miss the final. But when the fever broke, Holman raced to the Garden and arrived shortly before game time. As it turned out, the Beavers needed their coach's guile. Bradley took an early lead, as CCNY missed a number of easy shots. The flow of the game prompted Holman to switch from his fastbreak attack to more of a ball-control plan. It worked, and the Beavers' patience paid off. With two minutes left, they had a 64-61 lead.

There was a rule that year that called for a jump ball after every foul shot in the final minutes of a game. Bradley began to foul, hoping that the Beavers would miss the shots and that six-foot, seven-inch Elmer Behnke could control the tap against six-foot, three-inch Ed Warner. But it was Warner who prevailed, controlling the tap seven consecutive times, as CCNY took the NIT title with a 69-61 victory.

But it wasn't over yet. As was the custom then, NIT teams could then go on to the NCAA championship, which began later. Sure enough, the Beavers received a bid, and Holman decided to take his team after an unprecedented double triumph. Victories over Ohio State, 56-55, and North Carolina State, 78-73, put CCNY into the final. As fate would have it, the Beavers were once again pitted against Bradley. The Braves, too, had taken an NCAA bid and had beaten UCLA and Baylor en route to the finals.

As in the NIT, the two teams battled closely. The lead changed hands several times in the early going before City College took a 39-32 halftime advantage. But Bradley battled back once more, and in the closing minutes the Braves put on a full court press that seemed to rattle the usually imperturbable Beavers. Several steals and subsequent hoops cut the lead to a single point, 69-68. Then, with time running out, Bradley's Gene Milchiorre stole the ball once again. A basket here would put the Braves in front.

Melchiorre went up for the shot — but it was blocked by Irwin Dambrot. The ball was shuffled to Norm Mager, who went in for a layup to ice the game and the championship for the Beavers 71-68. CCNY had done it. They had won both the NIT and NCAA championships in the same season. And they had accomplished both before packed houses at Madison Square Garden, their home court. Nothing, absolutely

OPPOSITE: *Nat Holman holds the 1950 NIT trophy while congratulating MVP Ed Warner. CCNY would go on to win the NCAA title.*

BELOW: *City College in action against Bradley in the 1950 NCAA finals. The club won the game 71-68, making the only NIT-NCAA double victory in history.*

nothing, could have been more satisfying. Perhaps Nat Holman summed it up most accurately when he said: "It took us an hour to play each game, but it will take a lifetime to forget them."

Unfortunately, something else was about to happen that would also take a lifetime to forget, especially since there would be graphic reminders at various intervals from time to time. From what might have been college basketball's finest hour to that time, the sport was about to sink into its deepest abyss. For just around the corner was an event that would totally tarnish CCNY's incredible triumph, as well as the overall integrity of the college game.

BELOW: *Ed Warner (8) of City College grabs a rebound in front of Bradley's Charles Grover (14) during the NCAA finals. Warner had 14 points in the title game, while teammate Irwin Dambrot had 15 and was named the MVP.*

OPPOSITE: *It's yet another joy ride for coach Nat Holman following his CCNY team's unprecedented double victory. City College defeated Bradley in both the NIT and NCAA finals. But the joy would be short-lived, as the spectre of scandal sat just over the horizon.*

SCANDAL AND RECOVERY

In 1950-51 the college game was busy celebrating another successful season when the first ripples of a dark undercurrent began to appear. CCNY's unprecedented "double" was still hot news, especially in the New York area, while the All-American team sported such exciting players and future pro stars as Bob Cousy of Holy Cross, Paul Arizin of Villanova and Bill Sharman of Southern California.

Gambling, legal or otherwise, has always been a fact of American life. And sports, being a contest between individuals or teams, is a natural forum for betting, whether it be a friendly wager between friends or something more. The presence of bookmakers, big time gamblers and the so-called underworld in sports has always brought fear and concern to those who want to see sport remain clean.

The most famous sports-gambling scandal, of course, was the infamous "Black Sox" scandal of 1919, when a group of gamblers attempted to "fix" the 1919 World Series by offering several members of the Chicago White Sox bribes to throw the series to the underdog Cincinnati Reds. The result was the banishment for life of a number of White Sox players from the game of baseball and a black mark on the sport that lingered for many years.

By the 1940s betting on basketball games had become more than a matter of who would win and who would lose. Gamblers and bookmakers took to setting a "point spread," which gave the underdog some extra points with which to work. If the spread was nine points, for instance, the favorite would have to win the game by more than nine points for those betting on that team to win. If the favorite won the game, but by less than the nine-point spread, those betting

on the underdog would win their bets despite the fact that the team still lost the game.

Get it? The gamblers did. It didn't take much for some wiseguy to figure an angle. What if we got to a couple of players on a normally strong team and asked them to help us out? They wouldn't have to throw the game, but just go easy, make sure their team didn't cover the spread. A bad pass here, a blown layup there, a miss on a crucial free throw. That was something the good player could do without creating suspicion. And in doing so he could "shave" the necessary few points to enable his team to blow the spread. Easy as pie.

With this philosophy, it shouldn't be surprising that college players would be approached. After all, many of them were kids from poor backgrounds who could use a few extra dollars. And so what if they shaved a few points? Their teams would still win the games, and who would be hurt except the poor saps who plunked their money down hoping to make a killing? They were being greedy anyway.

There were rumors of this sort of attempted maneuver on and off throughout the early 1940s. Then, in 1945, a story broke that five members of the Brooklyn College basketball team had each taken $1000 to lose a game with Akron College that was scheduled for Madison Square Garden. The players were allegedly to receive another $2000 after the deed was done. However, one regular named Bill Rosenblatt would not cooperate, and when word of the fix leaked out the game was cancelled. The two men who tried to arrange the fix were caught and eventually sentenced to a year in jail. In the meantime, the five Brooklyn College players were expelled from school.

But that wasn't the end of it. Phog Allen, the longtime coach at Kansas, had often warned that Madison Square Garden was ripe for illegal doings, yet Allen's, as well as other warnings, were largely ignored. Then, in 1949, a George Washingon University player reported that gamblers had approached him about throwing a game, in addition to playing with the point spread. This revelation resulted in several arrests by New York District Attorney

OPPOSITE ABOVE: *A pair of New York City detectives help to book Daniel Lamont (center) on bribery charges involving an NYU basketball game.*

OPPOSITE LEFT: *There were ripples of scandal as early as 1945, when two men were accused of trying to fix a Brooklyn College game.*

ABOVE RIGHT: *Arthur Hicks was one of several Seton Hall players questioned by District Attorney Frank Hogan about a possible fix.*

RIGHT: *District Attorney Hogan (right) thanks Dave Shapiro of George Washington U for reporting a bribe attempt in 1949.*

Frank Hogan. Four men, all known gamblers, received short prison terms for their part in the attempted bribe.

Even with this example, little more was done to curb open betting at large arenas such as the Garden. In fact, the point spreads were often splashed all over the newspapers and were widely known by the coaches and players alike. It was even obvious at some games that many of the fans weren't cheering for the winning team, but seemed only interested in whether the point spread was being covered or not. It was also no secret that considerable sums of money were changing hands after the games. Finally, during the early weeks of 1951, the basketball finally hit the fan, and this time the spectre of large-scale gambling could not be ignored.

It began when a Manhattan College player named Junius Kellogg reported that he had been offered a $1000 bribe to make sure his team lost an upcoming game with De Paul by at least ten points. The person who did the offering was a former player, one of the co-captains from the year before. Kellogg, who happened to be the first black player at Manhattan, was stunned. He was also told that the former co-captain and another player had actually thrown three games the year before, had made $5000 each and had not come close to being caught.

Not wanting to jeopardize himself or his family, Kellogg went to Jaspers' coach Ken Norton, who alerted the Manhattan district attorney's office. Shortly after the game took place, with Manhattan winning, the gamblers and two former players were arrested. When all the facts were known, even those directly involved with the game realized how easy it would be for a couple of players to shave points or even throw a game.

Yet even with Kellogg's revelations and the subsequent convictions, college authorities were slow to react. Maybe they were simply hoping that the Manhattan episode would be the end of it. No such luck. A short time later Max Kase, the veteran sports editor of the *New York Journal-American*, was told by a bookmaker about a former college star acting as a go-between for gamblers who wanted to approach players in order to offer bribes. Kase immediately

ABOVE: *Ed Roman of City College (second from left) and Harvey Schaff (right) of NYU are about to be booked on bribery charges. Roman admitted to taking bribes, while Schaff was accused of offering them.*

RIGHT: *Former LIU player Dick Feurtada (right) is arrested after having been accused of throwing four games, as the basketball scandals continued to spread in the spring of 1951.*

went to District Attorney Hogan, and the subsequent investigation shocked the college basketball world. The number of players and schools involved in the illegal doings was astounding.

Hogan's investigation revealed that some 86 games in 23 cities had been fixed between 1947 and 1950 by 32 players from seven colleges. The schools involved were LIU, NYU, Manhattan, Bradley, Toledo and two shockers, Kentucky and City College of New York! It was bad enough that the first five were involved, but CCNY had just completed its amazing NIT-NCAA double, while at Kentucky, Adolph Rupp had publically bragged that the gamblers "couldn't touch my boys with a ten-foot pole."

The edifice of college basketball was crumbling. A former LIU player named Eddie Gard was one of the first arrested. He had been acting as a go-between to find players who would cooperate with the gamblers. As it turned out, Gard

ABOVE: *CCNY star Ed Warner's face shows concern after he was questioned by DA Hogan about possible fixed games. Warner and a number of his teammates were later arrested and admitted to taking money to throw three games during the great 1949-50 season.*

had been the one to contact members of Holman's CCNY team. That club was on a train from Philadelphia, returning from a victory over Temple, when the coach was informed that the DA's office would be picking up three of his players for questioning. The only thing the shocked coach could advise his players to do was tell the truth.

The three players were Ed Roman, Al Roth and Ed Warner, and when they finally told the truth after hours of intense questioning, the more complete picture began to emerge. The trio had taken bribes to dump three games the season before. Now Nat Holman knew why his team had the mysterious slump that almost prevented it from entering the tournaments it ultimately won.

It was also learned that Gard had been the go-between and had been representing Salvatore Sollazzo, a jewelry manufacturer and former convict. The contacts had been made over the summer, when hundreds of players flocked to the

Catskill Mountains to play for the various hotels in summer leagues. There, the players were wined and dined and given a taste of the good life, with the promise of more.

The whole thing had started in 1950 when Gard and another LIU teammate, Adolph Bigos, took money from Sollazzo for losing a game to North Carolina State. When teammate Sherman White, a top pro prospect, guessed what was happening, he too became part of the scheme. Despite the fact that Clair Bee's team that year won its first 16 games, some were unexpectedly close. And when the longtime coach learned what had happened, some friends thought the shock might literally kill him. As it turned out, he was a broken man, so great was the disappointment of what his boys had done.

More players were arrested. Floyd Layne, another CCNY player, admitted taking $3000 to shave points in a pair of games played at the Garden. Soon after, three more CCNY players — Irwin Dambrot, Norm Mager and Herb Cohen — were arrested and admitted they had taken money. Then three more LIU players were charged with similar offenses dating back to 1948. Two bookmakers, William Rivlin and Eli Klukofsky, were also arrested for having arranged the 1948 fix.

The scandal continued to spread. Ironically, most of the players hadn't even spent the money; they just had it stashed. And while most of the early wrath was directed at New York and Madison Squre Garden, with many teams voting to avoid the Big Apple and its showcase arena, the long arm of the law also began reaching out for them. Four of Bradley's five starters, all-American Gene Melchiorre among them, were accused of taking bribes to fix games, two of them at Bradley's own field house, not at the Garden.

The fallout continued. By autumn another bombshell exploded when it was revealed that Adolph Rupp's great Kentucky team of 1949 had also been involved. All-Americans Alex Groza and Ralph Beard, along with Dale Barnstable admitted splitting $2000 to shave points in the NIT that year against Loyola. But in trying to keep the score close, the game got away, and Loyola pulled off a gigantic upset. And while the players admitted only that one transgression, the DA's office in Lexington said that almost every game the team played all season involved gambling of some sort.

Groza and Beard would pay a heavy price. They were already NBA stars and part owners of the Indianapolis Olympians. But when news of the bribes surfaced they were immediately banned from the NBA for life by commissioner Maurice Podoloff, their pro careers over, their lives put on hold. And it didn't end there for Adolph Rupp. He would soon learn that a former Kentucky player named Jim Line had acted a go-between and had offered bribes to Walter

Hirsch and Rupp's newest star, seven-footer Bill Spivey. Hirsch was convicted on a fix charge, and while Spivey was only indicted on perjury charges, he too would never have the opportunity to play pro ball.

The far-reaching scandal also showed that some colleges had changed the records and transcripts of ballplayers just to get them admitted and had fed them a steady diet of easy courses to keep them eligible. The entire system had really come under indictment.

Fixers like Salvatore Sollazzo received stiffest sentences, while a few players, such as Sherman White, Ed Warner and Al Roth, received minor prison terms of six months to a year. The others received suspended sentences, but that didn't erase the permanent black mark on their lives; that would stay with them for years and years. And their names would forever be associated with what had become college basketball's darkest hour. There would be other scandals involving point shaving and dumping, but this was the first and remains the best remembered.

OPPOSITE BELOW: *In July of 1951 the scandal continued to spread. DA Hogan said that three Toledo University players had admitted taking money from a New York gambler. Photographed after being questioned were, left to right, Carlo John Muzi, Robert McDonald and William Walker.*

RIGHT: *Al Roth (left) of CCNY and Harvey Schaff of NYU are booked on charges of bribery in February of 1951.*

BELOW: *Kentucky's great All-American guard Ralph Beard was twice named Player of the Year by the National Assn of Basketball Coaches. He and teammate Alex Groza were on their way to great pro careers with the Indianapolis Olympians when they were accused in the scandal investigation in the fall of 1951. They admitted taking money to "shave" points in a 1949 NIT game against Loyola. Both were immediately banned from the NBA for life.*

Judge Saul S Streit of the court of general sessions, who heard a good deal of the case, also knew that the responsibilities did not just lie with a select few bad apples. Said Judge Streit: "The responsibility for the sports scandal must be shared not only by the crooked fixers and corrupt players, but also by the college administrations, coaches and alumni groups who participated in this evil of commercialism and overemphasis."

But would a lesson be learned? Like everything else, changes would only come by degrees. Much of what led to the scandal remained, and that's why it had happened again since. Perhaps it was those directly involved who really learned how disastrous the scandal has been. As one player whose life was ruined said later: "Tell any others who are tempted to do what I did to look at me. I'm a fine example. I did it because I wanted to be grown up. Sounds funny, doesn't it? I mean I was sick and tired of asking my father for money all the time."

The spectre of the scandal hung heavy over the college game as the 1950-51 season came to an end. Kentucky won the NCAA title in a new, expanded, 16-team field. The Wildcats, led by Bill Spivey before he was charged with perjury, defeated Kansas State 68-58 in the finals, which, because of the scandals, had been moved from Madison Square Garden to Minneapolis, Minnesota. Brigham Young won the NIT, defeating Dayton, but the victories had a hollow ring to them in 1951. The game itself was suspect.

But as in baseball's Black Sox Scandal, it would be the players who would bring the sport back. In the case of baseball it was the emergence of one man, Babe Ruth, who, by virtue of his long home runs, would entice the fans to return as well as putting some joy and excitement back into a tarnished game.

With college basketball it would be a kind of resurgence by committee. A host of outstanding players would emerge over the next decade, and they would excite the fans and elevate the game to a new and entertaining level. While their emergence could not completely erase what had happened in 1950, it would at least once again show fans the potential greatness of a sport that was still in the development stage, at least from a purely athletic standpoint. The new players would be bigger, stronger, faster and more agile. They would shoot better, jump higher and be more innovative and creative on the court. In other words, they were the generation that would truly bring basketball into the modern era.

Just consider the names of all-American players who would be competing throughout the decade of the 1950s: Cliff Hagen, Clyde Lovellette, Dick Groat, Tom Gola, Frank Selvy, Bob Pettit, Bill Russell, Sihugo Green, Rod Hundley, Tom Heinsohn, Wilt Chamberlain, Elgin Baylor, Oscar Robertson, Guy Rodgers, Jerry West, Jerry Lucas. These are just a few, the cream of the crop, players who went from great college careers to great careers in the pros. But there were players right behind them who also made huge contributions in the years following the scandals.

At the outset of the post-scandal period, it was the little men who made the headlines. Dick Groat, a six-foot guard from Duke, led the nation in scoring in 1951 and set a three-year mark in the process. Groat might have become an outstanding pro had he not decided to play baseball, where he became a star shortstop for the Pittsburgh Pirates.

A year later the country marveled at the exploits of Johnny and Eddie O'Brien, a pair of five-foot, nine-inch twins playing for Seattle University. As a junior in 1951-52,

Johnny O'Brien became the first collegian to score more than 1000 ponts in a season. He also played center in an exhibition game against the Harlem Globetrotters in which he scored 43 points, prompting Trotter star Goose Tatum to remark: "That Johnny O, he's not a little man, he's a big man."

But it was another truly big man who dominated the NCAA playoffs that year. He was a six-foot, nine-inch, 270-pound, barrel-chested center for the University of Kansas named Clyde Lovellette. Big Clyde was a bull, and it was his 33 points in the final game against St John's of New York that gave the already legendary Phog Allen his first championship in 32 years of coaching. Lovellette also finished his senior year by breaking Groat's three-year scoring record with 1888 points. (Groat had 1886.) But this was just the beginning of what would be a real record-setting decade.

The NIT in 1952 had a new champion in LaSalle of Philadelphia. What was notable about the final was the dominance of a six-foot, six-inch freshman named Tom Gola, who scored 22 points and shared the MVP prize.

A year later the scoring record would fall again, as John O'Brien completed his Seattle career with 2537 points in 99 games. Yet the scoring leader for the year was a six-foot, three-inch junior guard from Furman named Frank Selvy, who averaged 29.5 points per game, including a high of 63 against Mercer. The following year he would make those numbers look anemic with what he would accomplish. Indiana was the NCAA champion, with a one-point victory over Kansas, while Seton Hall, led by six-foot, 11-inch Walter Dukes, defeated St John's in the NIT final.

It was a time when individuals were beginning to attract as much attention as teams: The new players were that good. In 1953-54, for instance, Frank Selvy rewrote the college record book. The son of a Kentucky coal miner, he would have seemed a natural to join Adolph Rupp at Kentucky. But Selvy stood just five-feet, four-inches as a high school freshman and didn't even make the team until he was a junior. And when he graduated as a six-footer, Rupp still considered him too small for the Wildcats. So instead, he went to Furman in Greenville, South Carolina, where he became an all-American.

Though he was outstanding as a junior, he was even more devastating as a senior, averaging an unheard of 41.7 points per game. And on 13 February 1954, in a game against Newberry College, Selvy did something that most basketball fans still thought was impossible. With his parents in the stands, as well as many of his friends and neighbors, Selvy was primed for a big game. It was also the first basketball game to be televised in South Carolina.

By the end of the first quarter Selvy had 24 points. He added 13 more in the second, for a total of 37 by halftime. That, in itself, was a new NCAA mark. Then in the third period his teammates began feeding him even more. He tossed in another 25 to give him 62, and now the question was, how high could he go? Furman was letting Newberry shoot almost at will so it could get the ball back and feed it to Selvy. The strategy was working. Selvy was popping and hitting from all over the court.

He broke Bill Mlkvy's record of 73 points for a single game and kept going. With just 35 seconds left, Selvy had 90 points. Amazingly, he got eight more in the next 30 seconds, and with the clock ticking down, he had the ball once more. Double-teamed, he took a desperation shot just inside the half court line. Swish. The ball went in, and Frank Selvy had scored 100 points in a basketball game.

Another top star of 1953-54 was Bob Pettit of Louisiana State University. Pettit was a six-foot, nine-inch workhorse who never stopped trying to improve his game. He averaged 31.4 points a game in 1954, and while his scoring was eclipsed by that of Selvy, he was definitely one of the new stars of the game, as well as the man who put LSU basketball on the map. Pettit was a late-bloomer who had to work very hard to hone his game. He later said one of the big reasons was the lack of basketball influences in the South at that time. "What hurt back then was that none of the pro games were on television," Pettit said. "None of us really followed pro ball at all and knew nothing about it. That being the case, there were no real early influences and no one to copy, so I just pretty much learned the game through trial and error as I grew."

More and more youngsters were working as hard as Bob Pettit and becoming outstanding players. A perfect example was Tom Gola, who, as a freshman in 1952, had led La Salle to a NIT title. Now, in 1954, he had the Explorers on the verge of an NCAA championship. Kentucky had appeared to be the top team once again, sailing through a

OPPOSITE ABOVE: *Dick Groat of Duke is best remembered as a fine shortstop with the Pittsburgh Pirates. But he was also a great basketball All-American who set a three-year college scoring mark and led the nation in scoring in 1951.*

OPPOSITE LEFT: *The scandal of the early 50s left a mark on the college basketball scene. What led to the sport's comeback was the number of great players coming on to the college courts during the next few years. They began to play a brand of ball that had never been seen before. Two of the best were Sihugo Green of Duquesne and Tom Gola of LaSalle. Both were All-Americans who went on to fine professional careers.*

RIGHT: *Six-three Frank Selvy went to Furman University, where he broke many scoring records. Selvy averaged 41.7 points as a senior in 1954 and once scored 100 points in a single game.*

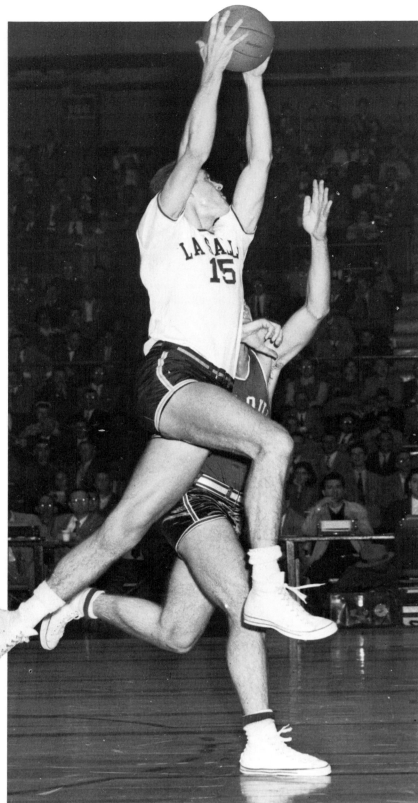

ten years in the NBA. If I had sat in the pivot I could have been like Dickie Hemrich or a lot of smaller guys who never made it in the pros."

Gola was a player who was prepared for just about everything. In the NCAAs of 1954 he had some incredible stats. Against North Carolina State he had 26 points and 26 rebounds. In a victory over Navy he tallied 22 and retrieved 24. And in the final against Bradley Gola scored 19 points, as La Salle took the title 92-76. Tom Gola was the tourney's

25-game schedule without a loss, and that included a victory over La Salle in the Wildcats' Christmas tournament. But right before the NCAA tourney was to start, Kentucky stars Frank Ramsey, Cliff Hagen and Lou Tsiropoulas were deemed ineligible because they had already earned enough credits to graduate. So the Wildcats couldn't compete.

That opened up the field and once again gave the six-foot, six-inch Gola a chance to shine, and Tom Gola was a ballplayer who could do it all. He was technically a center who twice led the nation in rebounding and even today holds the NCAA record for total career rebounds with 2201. As his coach at La Selle, Ken Leoffler, said, "I've never seen any one player control a game by himself the way Gola does."

But it was Leoffler's system that helped make Gola the complete player who easily made the transition to guard in the NBA. "At La Salle we played a five-man weave," Gola said. "Anybody could bring the ball up, and we all had places to go on the court. We had nobody sitting in the pivot, and the middle was always open to drives if you got by your man. So that's how I learned to handle the basketball, shoot from the outside and eventually play guard for

OPPOSITE LEFT: *Tom Gola in action against St Louis University in December of 1953. Gola led LaSalle to an NIT title as a freshman in 1952 and, at 6-6, led the nation in rebounding for two straight years.*

BELOW: *In 1954 Tom Gola again showed his greatness by leading LaSalle to the NCAA tile with a 92-76 win over Bradley. Here Gola gets two of his 19 points in the title game as he works his magic underneath.*

Most Valuable Player and an all-American selection for the third time in three years. He would be returning for one more go around in 1955.

Suddenly it seemed as if something new and exciting was happening in each successive season. The 1954-55 campaign brought to the fore a player destined to change both the college and, later, the professional game. He was Bill Russell, a six-foot, nine-inch center for the University of San Francisco. Russell wasn't a great ballhandler or great

shooter. And like many big men before him, it took him a couple of seasons to put his game together. But once he did, his presence enabled the Dons to control almost every game they played. For Bill Russell's game was defense. And he played with an intensity and determination that never relented. He became the game's premier shot blocker and rebounder. His presence under the hoop was an intimidating one. Many a player would pull up on a shot or alter its trajectory for fear that Russell would swoop down like a bird of prey and swat it away.

Complementing Russell's talents was a defensive-minded coach, Phil Woolpert, and a six-foot, one-inch guard with all-American talents, K C Jones. Russell was a junior in 1954-55 and since the team had been just 14-7 the year before, no one was prepared for what it was about to do. That record, however, was also a bit deceiving, since K C Jones missed most of the season after an appendicitis attack early

in the campaign and could not display his talents.

The Dons won their first two games of the year, then lost a 47-40 decision to UCLA. It would be the last defeat suffered by the Dons with Bill Russell in the middle. San Francisco swept through its next 21 games and into the NCAA championships. There Russell and the Dons defeated West Texas State and Utah easily and took a one-point victory over Oregon before heading to Kansas City for the Final Four.

In the semi-finals Russell scored 24, as San Francisco whipped Colorado 62-50. Then, in the finals, the Dons met Tom Gola and defending champion La Salle. The game was billed as a battle between Russell and Gola, but Woolpert put K C Jones on the La Salle star and allowed Russell to roam the middle. The strategy paid off, as San Francisco pulled away in the second half to win the title 77-63. Russell had 23 points and the MVP prize, while Jones surprised everyone with 24 points. And since there was no offensive goal

OPPOSITE ABOVE: *In 1955 a new era dawned when center Bill Russell led the University of San Francisco to the NCAA title. Russell was a 6-9 center who won games with defense and rebounding. In this 1955 semi-final NCAA game, USF's other all-American, K C Jones, scores as Russell (6) waits for a rebound.*

ABOVE: *Bill Russell shows his wingspan as he prepares to block a shot by Iowa's Bill Seaberg in the 1956 NCAA final. San Francisco won the title for a second straight year, as Russell scored 26 points to go with his shotblocking and rebounding.*

tending rule then, Russell also guided a number of teammates' shots into the hoop. It was a truly dominating performance.

And it was repeated again in 1955-56. Despite the fact that the rules committee widened the foul lane from six to 12 feet, Bill Russell was more effective than ever. The Dons won all 25 of their regular season games and went into the playoffs once again, this time with a winning streak of 51 consecutive games. Despite the fact that K C Jones was not eligible for the NCAA games, the Dons went all the way once more. This time they whipped Iowa in the final 77-63, with Russell scoring 26 points. The big guy would go on to even greater heights with the Boston Celtics of the NBA and would be joined by K C Jones and the other great Celtics stars. As for the Dons, their winning streak reached 60 games before the team lost to Illinois 62-33. The school would never achieve that level of greatness again.

The end of the 1956 season marked another milestone for the game. Phog Allen retired as coach at Kansas after 46 years and 771 victories. But the longtime basketball legend left something behind. One of his last battles was to recruit a mammoth seven-foot center from Overbrook High School in Philadelphia. His name was Wilt Chamberlain, and he was destined to become one of the giants of the sport, as controversial as he was talented.

Wilt was a sophomore playing his first varsity season in 1956-57, and as soon as he stepped on to a college court there were those who said his team would be unbeatable. As strong and well-coordinated as he was tall, Wilt was virtually unstoppable. In some ways he wasn't as intense or aggressive as Bill Russell, but he was bigger and stronger, and in the eyes of many, he played a better all-around game.

Sure enough, the Jayhawks were nearly unbeatable with Wilt in the lineup. The club lost only two games, and both opponents won by using deliberate stalling tactics which made for lousy basketball. But Kansas won the rest, with Wilt averaging some 30 points a game, and went into the NCAA tournament as co-favorites with the University of North Carolina. The Tar Heels, under coach Frank McGuire, were unbeaten in 27 games, and while they didn't have a dominating player of Chamberlain's caliber, they were a well-balanced, well-coached ballclub. Sure enough, when the smoke cleared it was the Tar Heels and the Jayhawks for the national title.

It turned into one of the greatest games in college basketball history. Carolina was led by the smooth-shooting, six-foot, six-inch Lenny Rosenbluth, but the Tar Heels also got mileage from six, nine Joe Quigg, six, six Pete Brennan and five, 11-inch Tommy Kearns. With Quigg and Brennan hitting from the outside, Carolina jumped to a 19-7 lead. Kansas began coming back behind Chamberlain, but McGuire countered by moving Rosenbluth into the pivot, and the thin forward responded with 14 points. Still, Kansas cut it to 29-22 by the half.

The second half was a battle royal. With Chamberlain shaking loose underneath, Kansas finally took the lead. They were up by three, with about 10 minutes left, when Jayhawk Coach Dick Harp went into a slowdown, almost a stall. Yet the game remained close. Rosenbluth fouled out with 1:45 left and 20 points. But a late shot by Bob Young enabled the Tar Heels to tie the game at 46 at the end of regulation play.

Both clubs were playing it cautious in the first overtime and traded just a single basket. It was tied at 48 as the second overtime began. Incredibly, neither team scored a single point in the second five-minute session. Now it was triple overtime, a rare occurrence anywhere and a first for the NCAA final. This time North Carolina looked to break it open with four quick points and a 52-48 lead. But Chamberlain and the Jayhawks came back. They tied it at 52-all, then took a 53-52 lead with just 31 seconds left.

Carolina tried desperately to get a hoop. With just six seconds left Joe Quigg was fouled while trying to convert a rebound. With the huge crowd at Kansas City's Municipal Auditorium watching in near silence, Quigg calmly sank both free throws, then slapped away a Kansas inbounds pass just before the buzzer sounded. North Carolina had won 54-53, to complete a 32-0 championship season.

As for Wilt Chamberlain, he was named the tourney MVP and returned again the next year. But with the defenses stacked against him, and teams playing all kinds of slowdowns and stalls to keep him from getting the ball, Kansas fell to 18-5 and failed to win its own conference title. Disgruntled, Chamberlain then left school and joined the Harlem Globetrotters for a year until he was eligible to enter the NBA, where his professional impact would be far greater than that of his college days.

OPPOSITE LEFT: *A new major force came on the college scene with the arrival of 7-1 Wilt Chamberlain at Kansas in 1956-57. The Big Dipper was unstoppable underneath but tired of smaller players beating on him and turned pro.*

ABOVE LEFT: *Elgin Baylor of Seattle was still another great college player who could do it all. And he was even better as a pro.*

ABOVE RIGHT: *Wilt towers over everyone in a 1956 Kansas win over California.*

As the decade of the 1950s neared its end more and more power players were entering the college ranks. A six-foot, five-inch forward named Elgin Baylor was already performing for Seattle University. Baylor was a do-everything kind of player who could shoot and rebound, as well as handle the ball. He was capable of going end to end, like a guard, and putting a variety of "moves" on his drives that often had his opponents shaking their heads in disbelief. His game was characterized by a seeming ability to hang in the air longer than his opponent, giving him the last move and, more often than not, another hoop. Of this ability newsman Emmett Watson once said: "He [Baylor] has never really broken the law of gravity, but he is awfully slow about obeying it."

Baylor and his Seattle team made it to the NCAA finals in 1958 but were beaten by another of Adolph Rupp's Kentucky teams 84-72, giving the Baron his fourth national championship. Baylor had 25 points in his final college game before joining the Los Angeles Lakers and going on to a brilliant pro career.

Two talented sophomores debuted in 1958 and would play with immense talent right through their college days and into the pros. They were Oscar Robertson at the University of Cincinnati and Jerry West at West Virginia. The Big O, as Robertson was called, was a six-foot, five-inch guard who could score and rebound with the best of them. In fact, Robertson was such a complete player, such a great all-around basketball star, that there are still people today who call the Big O the greatest ever.

Robertson didn't feel his way into the college game. He took it by storm. As a sophomore in 1957-58 he averaged 35.1 points a game to lead the nation in scoring. He would lead everyone for the next two seasons as well, becoming a three-time All-America in the process, and though his Bearcat team never made it to the NCAA finals, the Big O was perhaps the most respected player of his time. He is still the fourth leading all-time scorer in college basketball history, with 2973 points. As Wilt Chamberlain once said of

71

Oscar: "Oscar is not as fast as some ballplayers and not as good a shooter as others, but he knows how to put everything together better than anyone else."

Jerry West wasn't as big as Oscar Robertson, but at six-feet, three-inches he was plenty big enough to get the job done. West needed a season to get his game together, but by the time he was a junior in 1959 he was a bona fide all-American and one of the best clutch players ever. With the game on the line, the ball couldn't be in any better hands than Jerry West's. His clutch jumpers seemed to be guided by radar, and that was a trait he would carry over to his days as a pro with the Los Angeles Lakers.

At the end of the 1959 season both Robertson and West propelled their teams into the Final Four of the NCAA championships. But the Big O's Bearcats fell victim to the defensive-minded California Bears, coached by Pete Newell and featuring a six-foot, ten-inch center named Darrall Imhoff. California held the Big O to 19 points, whipping Cincinnati 64-58.

Meanwhile, West's Mountaineers were marching toward the finals, and much of the reason was Mr Clutch himself. In a second round game against St Joseph's of Philadelphia, West Virginia fell behind by a 67-49 score with just 13 minutes left. Incredibly, Jerry West took command and scored 21 points in just nine minutes. When the game ended West had 36 points and the Mountaineers had a 95-92 victory. After beating Boston College and Louisville, the Mountaineers were in the finals.

Once again West was brilliant, but the Bears had a more solid overall team that propelled them to a 12-point halftime lead. Then, in the second half, the Mountaineers went to Mr Clutch, and West responded. He led his club back and brought them to the brink of a national title. But West and the Mountaineers fell one point short, losing to California 71-70. West had scored 28 points and led everyone with 11 rebounds. His 160 points in five games earned him MVP honors, but it was defense that won it for the Bears.

Pete Newell, who coached California to the title, had a chance to assess both Robertson and West. He saw them both as great players. "I think Oscar was the tougher player in college," Newell said. "Both Oscar and Jerry played a lot of forward then, though Oscar handled the ball more. He was also a great passer, and when they would clear it out for him, there was no way to stop him one-on-one from penetrating and getting his shot. When Jerry became strictly a guard in the pros, he really improved his game, and then you couldn't stop him one-on-one, either. But in college Oscar was a little harder to defend because of the way he would go out and get the ball."

The 1959-60 season, which closed out college basketball's most turbulent decade, was also one of its greatest. Robertson and West were back for their senior year, as was California's Imhoff. But there was also a new star rising in the Midwest, and he would form the nucleus of a powerful team that would reach the NCAA finals three consecutive years.

His name was Jerry Lucas, a six-foot, eight-inch, 230-pound center who played the game the way it was supposed to be played. After breaking a slew of high school records, including Wilt Chamberlain's all-time scoring mark, Lucas turned down some 150 scholarship offers, which contained all kinds of promises, including a job for his father, to accept an academic scholarship to Ohio State. You see, he was also a straight-A student.

As a ballplayer he was completely unselfish, meshing his game to that of the team. And he could do it all — shoot, pass, and rebound. Though there were bigger and taller centers, he could out-rebound nearly all of them because of exquisite timing and anticipation. His shooting percentage was always over 60. Surrounded by a supporting cast that included John Havlicek and Larry Siegfried, Lucas and the Buckeyes became a powerhouse.

There wasn't anyone who questioned Lucas' overall ability. But perhaps it was North Carolina's Frank McGuire who voiced everyone's sentiments regarding the special

LEFT: *Toward the end of the 1950s more great players came. One of the best was Jerry West of West Virginia, a 6-3 forward-guard who could also do everything. Among other things he was a great clutch player who always wanted the ball at crunch time. He kept that trait right into his pro years with the LA Lakers.*

OPPOSITE: *There was only one Big O. Oscar Robertson was a three-time all-American at the University of Cincinnati, a player so talented that he has been called the best ever by many experts. Here he receives the Gold Star Award as the outstanding visiting basketball player in New York during the 1960 season. In fact, the Big O won the Gold Star for three straight years.*

GOLD STAR AW
OUTSTANDING VISITING
1959 - 60
THIRD CONSECUTIVE S
OSCAR ROBERTS
UNIVERSITY OF CINCIN
PRESENTED BY
METROPOLITAN BASKETBALL WRI   S'N

quality of the pivotman from Middletown, Ohio. "Lucas has the ideal attitude," McGuire said. "He'll play the post and pass off all day. If the team needs points, he'll get them. The rest of the time he passes off."

In the 1960 NCAAs both Robertson and West were taking their final shots at a national championship. But West Virginia lost in the second round to NYU, while Cincinnati lasted into the Final Four, only to be beaten in the semifinals once again by California 77-69. Ohio State cruised into the finals by whipping NYU 76-54. And then they won the title by an almost identical score, topping California easily 75-55, with Lucas scoring 16 points and grabbing ten rebounds.

By now the NCAA championships had become the prestige postseason tournament, since it determined the national champion. The NIT was still going strong at the Garden, but now it only got the teams that didn't make the

NCAA, and despite its great tradition, it would continue to diminish in importance as the years passed.

The decade of the 1950s was topped off by the choosing of an Olympic basketball team to represent the United States. On that team were Robertson, West, Lucas, Imhoff, Mel Nowell of Ohio State, Walt Bellamy of Indiana, Terry Dischinger of Purdue and several others. Guess who won? It was a team that probably could have won in the NBA.

There was little doubt now that college basketball had reached new heights. The great play of the superstars of the decade had all but erased the stigma of scandal. And while there would be another point shaving scheme uncovered in 1961, it wouldn't be as widespead as the first and wouldn't have the same damaging effect on the game. College basketball was too firmly established now. A few bad apples would always be there, but the glory of the game could now override any obstacles that might come its way.

OPPOSITE BELOW: *Ohio State's Larry Siegfried (dark jersey) scores a basket underneath as the Buckeyes top California 75-55 in the 1960 NCAA finals. Siegfried teamed with Jerry Lucas and John Havlicek to give Ohio State one of the nation's most feared teams.*

RIGHT: *Jerry West (left) and Oscar Robertson led an unstoppable US Olympic team to an easy gold medal in the 1960 games in Rome.*

BELOW: *Sam Stith (22) of St Bonaventure battles with Al Saunders of Bradley for a rebound during 1960 NIT action. The game was typical of the high quality of the sport played at the time. Number 31 is Bradley's Chet Walker.*

THE AGE OF THE BRUINS

ABOVE: *John Wooden, the well known Wizard of Westwood.*

LEFT: *Big Lew Alcindor from New York was Wooden's first great center. With the 7-2 Alcindor in the lineup, the Bruins took three straight NCAA championships.*

OPPOSITE ABOVE: *Cincinnati with Paul Hogue (22) upset Ohio State and Jerry Lucas (11) in the 1961 NCAA final.*

OPPOSITE RIGHT: *Bill Bradley of Princeton was one of the most exciting college stars of the early 1960s. Today he is a US Senator.*

At the outset of the 1960s it looked as if there might be a new Midwestern dynasty in college basketball, since the Cincinnati Bearcats went to the NCAA title game for three straight years, winning twice. But in 1964 there came a new champion from the West Coast. John Wooden's UCLA Bruins captured the NCAA title for the first time, but not for the last. In fact, before the Bruins were through they would win an unprecedented ten NCAA titles in 12 years, including seven in a row, creating a college basketball dynasty the likes of which has not been seen before or since. Coach Wooden would come to be called the Wizard of Westwood, and his teams would produce a succession of great players, the most well known being his two dominant centers, Lew Alcindor (later known as Kareem Abdul-Jabbar) and Bill Walton. But Wooden and the Bruins would also win without the big men, a further tribute to the coach and the fine players who came to Pauley Pavillion to play basketball.

It was the Bearcats of Cincinnati, however, who made the first big splash of the decade. Coach Ed Jucker's quintet, minus the graduated Oscar Robertson, made it to the NCAA finals from 1961 to 1963. A team without a superstar, the Bearcats surprised the basketball world by whipping Jerry Lucas, John Havlicek and their Ohio State teammates for the title those first two years by scores of 70-65 and 71-59. The players on those NCAA Bearcats teams are now largely forgotten, but under Jucker the likes of Ron Bonham, Bob Wiesenhahn, Paul Hogue, Tom Thacker and Tony Yates did the job as a team and won both years in big upsets. The next year, 1963, the Bearcats attempted to become the first team to win three NCAA titles in a row, but they were upended by a surprising Loyola of Chicago quintet 60-58 in overtime. The Cincinnati reign was over.

During this period, there were a number of other outstanding players thrilling the increasingly large crowds that were flocking to see college basketball. The all-American list included stars such as Tom Stith of St Bonaventure, Terry Dischinger of Purdue, Chet Walker of Bradley, Walt Bellamy of Indiana, Billy McGill of Utah, Len Chappell of Wake Forest, Art Heyman of Duke, Barry Kramer of NYU, Rod Thorn of West Virginia and Nate Thurmond of Bowling Green.

Then, in 1963-64, fans also began following the exploits of a brilliant student who played basketball for Princeton University. His name was Bill Bradley, and he would later become a pro star and then a United States Senator. Dave

Stallworth of Wichita State, Cotton Nash of Kentucky, Jeff Mullins of Duke, and Cazzie Russell of Michigan were other players attracting attention that year.

But the team to watch in 1963-64 was the UCLA Bruins. Their coach, John Wooden, had been the head mentor at the school since 1949, and while he had produced a number of winning teams, the veteran coach still hadn't brought the ballclub to national prominence. Wooden had been a three-time all-American at Purdue from 1930 through 1932 and still believed in a controlled yet fastbreaking offense, as well as a pressing, trapping defense. Coaching in close proximity to Phil Woolpert at San Francisco and Pete Newell at California, both of whom emphasized defense, Wooden must have felt like an orphan of the storm. But he persisted in sticking with the system in which he so strongly believed.

Then, in the early 1960s, he began going after and getting better ballplayers. In 1961-62 Wooden brought Walt Hazzard from Philadelphia to quarterback his small but quick team, and the Bruins surprised everyone by making the Final Four and nearly upsetting Cincinnati in the semi-finals. A year later guard Gail Goodrich and forward Keith Erickson arrived, and by 1963-64 Kenny Washington was there to perform as a sixth man off the bench. While Wooden didn't have a starter taller than six-feet, five, he proceeded to turn the college basketball world into UCLA's personal stage.

Wooden's fullcourt press was both devastating and a thing of beauty: Taller, slower teams simply could not cope with it. That was evident from the opening game of the 1963-64 season, when the Bruins easily rolled over Brigham Young by a score of 113-71, serving notice to everyone that they were a team to be reckoned with. In December they completely outclassed a powerful Michigan team led by Cazzie Russell and proceeded to sweep past the remainder of their opponents en route to a perfect 26-0 record. Now it was on to the NCAAs to prove it was all real.

The club had two close calls in the West Regional, getting past Seattle 95-90, then topping San Francisco by only four, 76-72. But they were on their way to the Final Four for the second time in two years and would be meeting Kansas State in the semi-finals. Once again it was a battle, and the Bruins needed a 28-point performance from Keith Erickson to win 90-84. Now they would be facing Duke in the finals. The Blue Devils had an all-American guard in Jeff Mullins, but perhaps more important, a pair of six-foot, ten-inch frontliners in Jay Buckley and Hack Tison. Could the Bruins cope with their height?

Sure enough, Duke used its height advantage to take the early lead, but late in the first half Wooden changed strategy. He went to a zone and sent Kenny Washington and Doug McIntosh into the game. The Bruins promptly reeled off 16 straight points and rolled from there, winning a 98-83 decision and their first national championship. Goodrich finished with 27 points, and Washington with 26, while Walt Hazzard was named MVP.

BELOW: *A pair of all-Americans, Walt Hazzard (42) of UCLA and Jeff Mullins (44) of Duke fight for a loose ball during the 1964 NCAA title game. The Bruins won 98-83, giving Coach Wooden the first of his ten championships.*

OPPOSITE: *By 1967, the age of Alcindor had arrived. In a December game against St Louis University, Alcindor goes high in the air to score on a sweeping hook shot. Bruin opponents everywhere spent three years asking the same question: How can we stop him?*

The next year the Bruins were back. Though they lost their opener 110-83 to Illinois, UCLA won 24 of its next 25 games. Now they were ready to defend their championship. Hazzard was gone, Mike Lynn and Edgar Lacey were the new forwards, while McIntosh was the center and Washington was still the sixth man. It was not a big squad, just fast and opportunistic. And they knew how to win.

Their fastbreak offense racked up some big scores, and in the NCAAs they whipped Brigham Young 100-76 and San Francisco 101-93, then worked their way into the Final Four to face Wichita State. With Goodrich hitting for 28 and Lacey 24, the Bruins won with fastbreaking ease 108-89. In the other semi-final, Cazzie Russell and Michigan had beaten Bill Bradley and Princeton 93-76, even though Bradley hit for 29 points.

Now it was the Bruins' speed against the Wolvernes' bulk. And this time the six-foot, one-inch Goodrich was the man of the hour, scoring 42 points to Russell's 28 as the Bruins won their second straight title 91-80. Goodrich probably would have been the MVP had not Bill Bradley shown his greatness once more in the consolation game against Wichita State. The future Rhodes Scholar scored an incredible 58 points in a Tiger victory to capture the Most Valuable Player prize.

In the fall of 1965 John Wooden showed everyone he was not necessarily dedicated to playing without big men. He went out and signed the biggest of the big, bringing Lew Alcindor, a seven-foot, two-inch center from New York's Power Memorial High to UCLA. Alcindor was one of the most sought-after schoolboy centers in years. He gave a foreshadowing of things to come when he led the UCLA freshmen team against the Bruin varsity, still considered one of the best quintets in the land. The first year players won easily, 75-60, but because freshmen couldn't play varsity back then, the rest of the college basketball world figured they had one more year to scramble for the championship. The three years after that would belong to Alcindor and UCLA.

The big guy certainly had the credentials. He was nearly six feet, four when he was 11 years old and had grown to six, six when he first played for Power Memorial. But unlike a lot of very tall boys he didn't really go through a clumsy, uncoordinated stage. He always knew how to play the game and had the skills to execute on the court. Power Memorial was 95-6 with Lew Alcindor in the center slot, and five of the six losses came when the big guy was a freshman. In all, Alcidor led his team to an incredible 71-straight victories. It's no wonder he had college recruiters drooling.

But perhaps more than anything else, Lew Alcindor was always a team player. He didn't worry about his scoring average, or getting his shots, or reading his press clipping. He wanted his team to win. That's what made him happy, and that's why John Wooden wanted him so badly. Wooden's clubs played team basketball; the coach would have it no other way. To have a player of Alcidor's obvious talents blend in with the rest of the team, well, you didn't have to be a genius to draw the obvious conclusions.

And that's why the 1966 NCAA championship was dubbed the "Last Chance Tournament." In plain English, it would be the last chance for any of the other top teams in the country to garner the NCAA title before Alcindor and the Bruins cornered the market. And that's exactly the way it happened.

While the Bruins had an off year in 1965-66, a number of other teams joined the scramble. The most surprising of these clubs was Texas Western, now called Texas-El Paso. The Miners surprised everyone with a 23-1 record and a third place national ranking. To reach the Final Four, the Miners had to win an overtime game against Cincinnati and a double-overtime contest against Kansas. They were joined by top-ranked Kentucky, second-ranked Duke and surprising Utah. But three of the nation's top four teams were in the Final Four, and each knew this would have to be the year.

There was some popular sentiment in favor of Adolph Rupp and Kentucky. The veteran coach was back to try for

OPPOSITE FAR LEFT: *An aging Adolph Rupp was still in charge of Kentucky basketball fortunes in 1966.*

OPPOSITE LEFT: *Guard Gail Goodrich was a UCLA fixture for three years and was an all-American.*

ABOVE: *Coach Don Haskins (left) and members of his Texas Western team share the 1966 NCAA title trophy after upsetting Kentucky in the final 72-65. It was the year last before Lew Alcindor started play for UCLA.*

the fifth NCAA title, and the Baron wanted it badly. When the Wildcats just got by Duke and its tough tandem of Bob Verga and Jack Marin 83-79, they were in the finals. There they would be facing the surprising Miners, who had topped Utah 85-78.

It was a strange matchup. The Baron's Kentucky team didn't have a starter over six-feet, five and were nicknamed Rupp's Runts. Texas Western was led by the likes of David Lattin, Bobby Joe Hill, Orsten Artis, Willie Worsley, Willie Cager and Neville Shed — not exactly household names, but under Coach Don Haskins, the team had really jelled. They could score, rebound and play defense.

In the final the Miners proved just a little bigger, a little faster and a little better than Kentucky, which was led by Louie Dampier, Larry Conley and Pat Riley, who would later become the coach of the Los Angeles Lakers of the 1980s. Texas Western had the lead all the way and won it 72-65. Still, in the minds of many it was a no-name tournament. They point to the fact that the MVP prize was won by Utah's Jerry Chambers, who scored 143 points in four games. Yet Chambers' club lost both of its Final Four con-

tests. But never mind, Alcindor and his new teammates were about to make their presence felt.

When 1966-67 opened basketball fans saw just how carefully John Wooden had recruited and assembled his team. The Bruins varsity would feature four sophomores and a junior. Mike Warren, a cat-quick point guard, was the junior starter. Joining him were Alcidor at center, six-foot, seven-inch Lynn Shackelford, who had a deadly shot from the corner, Ken Heitz, who was only a shade over six, three, but was an outstanding defender and team player, and Lucius Allen, a six-foot, three-inch shooting guard who came from Kansas.

The team served notice in its very first game of the season, walloping Southern California 105-90. In that contest Alcindor scored a team record of 56 points: It was his first taste of varsity action. As the Bruins continued to roll over opponent after opponent, teams tried everything to stop them. The stall seemed the best weapon. Midway through the season Southern Cal tried it. Playing a rematch of the opener and using a completely different strategy, the Trojans almost pulled an upset. But UCLA nevertheless won 40-35.

To the surprise of no one, the Bruins finished the regular season with a perfect 26-0 mark and opened the NCAA tourney as heavy favorites. And why not? Alcindor had more than lived up to expectations, with a 29-point scoring average and nearly complete dominance over his opponents. He would also set an NCAA mark by hitting on 66.7 percent of his shots from the field. At the same time, Warren, Allen and Shackelford all averaged in double figures, with the two guards playing at almost an all-American level.

LEFT: *In one of college basketball's real classics the Houston Cougars, led by 6-9 Elvin Hayes (44), stopped UCLA's 47-game win streak 71-69. Hayes scored 39 points in the 20 January 1968 game that was played before some 55,000 fans in the Houston Astrodome.*

OPPOSITE RIGHT: *Lew Alcindor has the net around his neck after the Bruins took another NCAA title in 1969. The big guy had 37 points in this one.*

OPPOSITE RIGHT: *Lew Alcindor scores over the outstretched hand of North Carolina's Bill Bunting in the 1968 NCAA final. Alcindor, as always, couldn't be stopped and scored 34 points.*

OPPOSITE FAR RIGHT: *At 5-9, they said Niagara's Calvin Murphy was too small. But the Connecticut native proved everyone wrong, averaging more than 30 points a game for two straight years, and then going on to stardom in the NBA.*

The NCAAs seemed like exhibition games for the Bruins. They whipped Wyoming 109-60, then topped Pacific 80-64 to reach the Final Four. There they easily defeated the University of Houston, despite the presence of its all-American forward, Elvin Hayes, 73-59. And in the finals against a Cinderella Dayton team and all-American Donald May the Bruins prevailed with a 79-64 victory, as Alcindor had 20 points and 18 rebounds. It was Wooden's and the Bruins' third national title in four years, and with the entire team returning the following season, it was hard to see anyone beating them.

But even the Bruins were human. They had to sweat out their opener, with a clutch jumper by reserve Bill Sweek en-

abling them to top Purdue at the buzzer 73-71. After that they rolled again until their win streak reached 47 games. That's when they had a rematch with Houston and Elvin Hayes. The Big E, as he was called, was in his senior year and was a six-foot, nine powerhouse. He and the Cougars were unbeaten in 17 games, and their match with the Bruins was for the number one ranking in the country. On top of that, the game would be played in the Houston Astrodome, where more than 50,000 fans were expected to produce the largest gate in basketball history.

There was just one problem. Lew Alcindor was not 100 percent. The big guy had suffered a scratched eyeball some eight days earlier and had spent several nights in the hospi-

tal. He had only practiced once and had received clearance to play just a day before the scheduled game. He could have sat it out, but he wanted to be in there.

It turned out to be one of the great games in college basketball history. And to this day people who saw it still wonder if the outcome would have been different if Alcindor had not suffered the eye injury. He obviously was not himself, hitting on just four of 18 shots from the field.

Hayes, on the other hand, was unreal for most of the first half. The Big E tried to draw Alcindor away from the basket and couldn't miss, hitting one jump shot after another. By the end of the first half he already had 29 points. Yet even without their big man at full strength, the Bruins were making a game of it at 46-43.

With Hayes cooling in the second half, UCLA tied it at 54, but then the Bruins also went cold. Houston took the lead, only to have UCLA tie again at 65 and then at 69. But with less than 30 seconds left Hayes drove to the hoop, was fouled and converted both free throws. From there the Cougars held for a 71-69 victory, with Hayes scoring 39 points to Alcindor's 15.

It would be the only game the Bruins would lose all year. And when they went into the NCAA tournament at season's end they had their chance for revenge. Once again their semi-final opponent was Houston, and this time UCLA poured it on. They trampled the Cougars 101-69, and Hayes scored just 10 points. There was little doubt as to which was the better team. The final was almost a formality, as the Bruins defeated North Carolina 78-55, with Alcindor scoring 34 points.

Even with the loss of Warren and Allen in 1968-69, it was more of the same. Alcindor and his teammates were unbeaten until the final game of the season, when Southern Cal upset them. But in the tourney it was all Bruins, as they

roared into the finals and then easily topped Purdue 92-72. Alcindor, in his final game as a collegian, scored 37 points and grabbed 20 rebounds. More important, he had made all those predictions come true, leading the Bruins to an NCAA title in each of his three seasons. It was also Wooden's fifth title in six years, a record that would stand even if the veteran coach never won another. But he wasn't about to stop there.

Though the years from 1966 to 1969 can accurately be termed The Alcindor Years, big Lew and his Bruin teammates weren't the only things happening in college basketball. Though no school could match the Bruins in terms of total team power, the ranks were nevertheless filled with outstanding basketball players who provided countless hours of entertainment for their fans.

Besides Alcindor and Hayes, some of the all-American players at this time included guards Jim Walker of Providence, Clem Haskins of Western Kentucky, Bob Verga of Duke, Pete Maravich of LSU, Larry Miller of North Carolina, Rick Mount of Purdue and Calvin Murphy of Niagara. The best of the big men were Wes Unseld of Louisville, Spencer Haywood of Detroit, Mel Daniels of New Mexico, Bob Lanier of St Bonaventure and Dan Issel of Kentucky.

Walker of Providence was a senior in Alcindor's sophomore season of 1966-67 and led the nation in scoring, with a 30.4 average, the only man to finish ahead of the UCLA star. Only a year earlier Walker had scored 50 points in a game against Boston College during the Madison Square Garden Holiday Festival. He could drive, rebound and stick the jumper with regularity, as well as control the pace of a ballgame.

The two other really notable guards were Niagara's Murphy and LSU's Maravich. Both were high scorers who could electrify the crowds. Murphy was a mighty mite at five feet, nine, who proved time and again that he could play with

bigger men. He was a cat-quick jump shooter and a strong player who wasn't afraid to mix it up inside. During the 1967-68 season the little guy averaged a very big 38.2 points a game. He then went on to an outstanding professional career.

Pistol Pete Maravich was in a class by himself. During his three varsity years at LSU he led the nation in scoring, setting 11 NCAA records. His scoring average in each of his three seasons was 43.8, 44.2 and 44.5 points per game. That gave him career average of 44.2, still another mark, as was his total of 3667 points. And, amazingly, he set still another standard by scoring 50 or more points in a game 28 times in his three-year career.

But scoring wasn't the only thing Pete Maravich did well. You see, Pete Maravich was something of a basketball phenomenon. Under the tutelage of his coaching father, Press, he prepped to be a basketball star all his life. And that meant literally living the sport 24 hours a day. Young Pete would dribble a ball wherever he went, even while sitting on the aisle in a movie theatre or leaning out the window of a car. He spent his summers at basketball camps with his father, and he spent his winters hanging around the college players whom his father coached.

When he arrived as LSU he was ready. Daddy Press was

the coach, and Pete was unleashed upon the basketball world as a sophomore in 1967-68. The Tigers never really had a strong team, but they still drew the fans because people wanted to see their one-man gang in action. Pete was an offensive machine, but in addition to his scoring, people came to see the things he could do with the basketball. He was a dribbling and passing wizard, who could easily go behind his back, between his legs or behind his neck. His deft passes often caught unsuspecting teammates unaware. And he himself called his version of the game "Showtime." As he once said, "If there was no one in the stands I wouldn't play."

Besides Alcindor and Hayes, the top big men were Unseld, Haywood and Lanier. Unseld was a strong six feet, eight inches and a player who believed in the team, in playing strong defense and rebounding. He wasn't as tall as a lot of big men, but he knew how to use his considerable bulk and his strength, and it not only made him a top player in college but in the professional ranks as well.

The six-foot, eight Haywood came out of nowhere to lead the United States basketball team to a gold medal in the 1968 Olympic Games. He subsequently entered the University of Detroit, where he became an all-American in his first year, then left to join Denver of the ABA, where he was an all-pro his rookie season.

Daniels and Issel were two other big men who would go on to fine pro careers, while the six-foot, 11-inch Lanier made tiny St Bonaventure a national power that could com-

pete with anyone. Big Bob also went on to a fine pro career as one of the NBA's premier centers.

But the college story continued to be UCLA. With the graduation of Lew Alcindor, and with no other big man in sight to replace him, the rest of the basketball world thought they might finally catch up with John Wooden's Bruins. But even without a dominant center the Wizard of Westwood had more than an ample amount of talented players ready to go, and, as usual, he was ready to put all the pieces together into a cohesive, winning unit.

Steve Patterson took over at center. He was a six-foot, nine-inch player who would work the high post. The Bruins also had a pair of outstanding forwards in six-foot, seven junior Curtis Rowe and six-foot, nine sophomore Sidney Wicks. John Vallely was the shooting guard, while speedy Henry Bibby served as the point guard, a point guard who could also shoot.

Though not the ultra-high scoring quintet of the Alcindor days, the 1969-70 Bruins were a hustling, scrapping team. They could no longer depend on the big guy, so everyone hit the boards and everybody scored. The result was more victories. Though the team lost to Oregan and Southern Cal during the course of the season, they nevertheless finished with a 24-2 record and were the number two team in the land. Now the question was, could they win a fourth straight NCAA title? One thing was certain. Their coach had a lot of faith in them. "This team gave me as much satisfaction as any team I coached," Wooden said. "We had a lot

OPPOSITE TOP: *Louisville's Wes Unseld, only 6-8, was one of the game's top centers. Here's Unseld (31) in action against Boston College during the 1966 NIT Tourney. He later became the NBA's top rookie and Most Valuable Player in the same year.*

OPPOSITE BOTTOM: *LSU's Pete Maravich confers with his coach, who happened to be his dad, Press. The 6-5 "Pistol" was the top scorer in college basketball in all three of his varsity seasons, averaging more than 44 points for his career and setting records that still haven't been broken. Pete lived basketball right into a great pro career and always put on an exciting show for the fans.*

RIGHT: *Spencer Haywood (8) took charge of a mediocre United States Olympic team in 1968 and led it to yet another gold medal.*

of close games, but they would always find a way to pull them out."

That magic might well be needed in the NCAAs, which featured a brace of good ballclubs. Kentucky, with Issel, came in as the top-rated team, but there would be competition from Notre Dame, with Austin Carr, Jacksonville, with seven-foot, two-inch Artis Gilmore, St Bonaventure, with Lanier, and the usual dark-horse teams. But a number of the top teams were log-jammed in the Mideast Regional and were knocking each other off. Jacksonville, averaging 100 points a game, upset Kentucky in the regional final 106-100, to reach the Final Four. St Bonaventure also made it, but in the East final against Villanova, Lanier injured a knee and could not play again.

UCLA, in the meantime, had an easy time of it in the West Regional, defeating Long Beach State and Utah State to reach the Final Four. In the semi-finals the Bruins whipped New Mexico State 93-77 and prepared to face Jacksonville, which had beaten Lanier-less St Bonaventure. The question now was whether the Bruins could contain the Dolphins' big men, the seven-foot, two-inch Gilmore, and seven-foot Pembrook Burrows.

Jacksonville had the advantage in the early going, but Wooden made some defensive adjustments and had the six-foot, nine-inch Wicks playing Gilmore. The strategy worked, and UCLA took the lead before the half. From there they worked to an 80-69 victory, stopping the Jacksonville

scoring machine and winning their fourth NCAA title in a row. Wicks had 17 points and 18 rebounds in the final and was named the MVP. But it was Curtis Rowe who called the turn on the 1970 champions. "For three years everybody always said Lew did it," the jubilant Rowe said. "Well, we just proved that four other men from that team could play basketball."

They could indeed, and a year later they were back, except for Vallely, and ready to do business again. Despite another spate of close games, the Bruins finished the 1970-71 season with a 25-1 record, the only loss being to Notre Dame, as the great Irish all-American Austin Carr scored 46 points. Then came the NCAAs again. It was beginning to look as if the Bruins owned the tournament.

An easy victory over Brigham Young was followed by a real scare from Long Beach State. Jerry Tarkanian's team used an effective zone and held the lead most of the way. But subs Larry Farmer and John Ecker came off Wooden's bench and rallied the Bruins to a 57-55 victory, putting them into the Final Four, which was to be held at the huge Astrodome in Houston, Texas.

The Bruins looked anything but devastating in defeating Kansas 68-60 in the semi-final, yet it was enough to land them in yet another final game, this time against Villanova and their six-foot, eight-inch all-American, Howard Porter. It was not an easy game. Wooden began with a zone press to slow down the Villanova running game, and the Bruins took the early lead, which they stretched to 45-37 by the half: One of the reasons was that center Steve Patterson was having one of the great games of his life. But in the second half Villanova began coming back, and it was Wooden who had his club go into a stall. The Wildcats cut the lead to four, then to three, with only two minutes left. As usual, however, UCLA reached back for that little something extra and went on to win 68-62 behind Patterson's 29 points to give Coach Wooden his fifth straight national championship, a record on top of a record.

With Rowe, Wicks and Patterson due for graduation, once again everyone wondered what John Wooden could do for an encore. Would the Bruins finally drop down into the rest of the pack, or would the Wizard of Westwood have more outstanding players ready to step in? Wooden suggested an answer to that question at a press conference he held shortly after he won his fifth straight NCAA title: He said he thought that his Bruins might be contenders again in 1972 because of a six-foot, 11-inch freshman center named Bill Walton.

Walton was almost a local kid, coming from nearby San Diego, and he matured quickly as a player. His Helix High School team had won 49 straight games, with the red-headed Walton busy in the pivot with a 29 point and 22 rebound average. Like Alcindor before him, Walton was a consummate team player, especially adept to starting the fastbreak off the rebound. His passing from the center slot was impeccable. Wooden couldn't have asked for anything more.

OPPOSITE LEFT: *Dan Issel was still another great player at Kentucky, though the Wildcats never bid for the national crown while he was at center. But the 6-9 Issel was a good one who later starred in the old American Basketball Assn, and later the NBA.*

ABOVE: *Notre Dame's Austin Carr (34) was one of the top college scorers. Among his feats was a 61-point performance in an NCAA game in 1970.*

TOP RIGHT: *After Lew Alcindor graduated, 6-9 Sidney Wicks led the Bruins to a pair of NCAA titles, helping UCLA bridge the gap between Alcindor and Bill Walton.*

But he had more. Forwards Keith Wilkes and Larry Farmer were both outstanding players, Bibby returned to lead the backcourt, and was joined by Greg Lee. There was also a solid bench, with Larry Hollyfield, Tommy Curtis and another six-foot, 11-inch center, Sven Nater, who would have been a starter with most other teams. Collectively, they rallied behind the big redhead and became known as the Walton Gang. And before they were through they would rack up a record-setting 88-game winning streak.

It started quickly and easily in 1971-72. The Bruins just rolled through the regular season schedule. They were unbeaten in 26 games, winning by an average victory margin of 30 points a contest. Though he played a different kind of game than Lew Alcindor, Bill Walton was just as dominating a center. He could score, but it was his rebounding and passing that really made the team go. Those skills were evident in the NCAA tourney, as the Bruins easily whipped Weber State and Long Beach State, priming them for the Final Four once again.

In the semi-finals they defeated Louisville, coached by former Wooden assistant Denny Crum, 96-77, with Walton scoring 33 points. In the finals they would be meeting a Cinderella Florida State team that had beaten Bob McAdoo and North Carolina 79-75. Before that, Florida State had also whipped Kentucky, in what proved to be the final game ever for Adolph Rupp. The Baron was retiring, and the Seminoles had prevented him from having a last hurrah.

But while they put up a good fight, the Seminoles were no match for the Bruins. UCLA had a 50-39 halftime lead and coasted in from there 81-76, with Walton scoring 24 and grabbing 20 rebounds. They had done it again, won the NCAA title for the sixth straight year, the eighth in the last nine years. The Bruins were proving to be an unparalleled basketball dynasty, and with Walton and his playmates back for two more seasons, it was difficult seeing anyone stopping them.

Only Henry Bibby had been lost to graduation the following year, and the Walton Gang took right up where it had left off the season before. They looked unbeatable. On 25 January the team defeated Loyola of Chicago for its 60th

OPPOSITE: *Big 6-11 Bill Walton was John Wooden's answer to the question of what UCLA would do for an encore in 1972. No coach could have asked for more.*

BOTTOM LEFT: *Denny Crum, with the traditional carnation, coaching Louisville in the NCAAs. Crum led his Cardinals to titles in 1980 and '86.*

BELOW: *UCLA's Henry Bibby shooting a jumper against Florida State in the 1972 championship game. Bibby scored 18 points in the title game.*

straight win, tying the all-time record set by Bill Russell's San Francisco teams nearly 20 years before. Two nights later they whipped nemesis Notre Dame to set a new mark. Now the question was, how far the streak would go?

By the time they arrived at the NCAAs the streak was at 71. The Bruins started their quest for seven straight with a 98-81 victory over Arizona State. San Francisco was next, and the Dons tried to play slowdown. But the Bruins still prevailed 54-39 and were once again, ho hum, in the Final Four.

It was getting so predictable. In the semi-finals they whipped a strong Bobby Knight Indiana team 70-59, then went into the finals against Memphis State, a team that featured a strong six-foot, nine-inch forward in Larry

ABOVE: *The UCLA machine went on rolling in 1972 with Big Bill Walton taking over at center. They were NCAA champs once more, as well as completing an unbeaten season. The Bruins tenacity can be seen in the title game against Florida State, as Larry Farmer (with ball), Henry Bibby (behind him) and Keith Wilkes all mix it up inside.*

OPPOSITE: *Bob McAdoo (35) was the big star of a North Carolina team that went to the NCAA semi-finals in 1972. The Tar Heels, under Coach Dean Smith, always put a strong team on the floor with fine, individual stars. But despite McAdoo's presence, the 1972 Tar Heels lost to Florida State by a 79-75 score.*

OPPOSITE: *Bill Walton (in dark jersey) was the ideal center. He was a team player, yet could score, rebound, pass, and block shots.*

RIGHT: *David Thompson was the leader of a North Carolina State team that downed Walton and UCLA in 1974. Thompson could leap to the sky and was college basketball's most dynamic player in '74.*

BELOW: *Forward Keith Wilkes was another UCLA all-American during the Walton years. He was so smooth he had the nickname "Silk."*

Kenon and a sharpshooting guard, Larry Finch. But on this day no one else would count besides Bill Walton.

Playing perhaps his finest all-around offensive game, the big redhead hit on 21 of his 22 field goal attempts, many of them in close, to score 44 points in leading the Bruins to still another championship 87-66. Walton was the MVP for the second straight year, and the Bruins' winning streak was still going at 75 straight. The big guy and his teammates had one more year, and perhaps now they would have the showdown that had not come in 1973.

You see, there had been another unbeaten team that year, but they had been barred from post-season play because of some NCAA violations. But North Carolina State, under Coach Norm Sloan, still promised to have something to say in 1973-74. The Wolfpack had a bone fide superstar all-American in six-foot, four-inch David Thompson, a sky-walker who could seemingly leap into the stratosphere. They also had a seven-foot, four center named Tom Burleson, who didn't have the skills of a Walton but who played hard and, by virtue of his size, effectively. The other player to watch was five-foot, seven Monte Towe, a darting guard who held his own against much bigger opponents.

With this stage set, the 1973-74 season proved to be one of the greatest ever. There was the drama of the UCLA win streak, the try for eighth straight NCAA title and the anticipated confrontation with North Carolina State. That would come early, because Coach Wooden had given his Bruins a rugged schedule that had them meeting both State and another Atlantic Coast Conference power, Maryland, early in the season. No one could accuse the Wizard of Westwood of looking for the easy way out.

With Larry Farmer graduated, junior Dave Meyers stepped in at forward to take up the slack. Wilkes and Lee were back to join Walton, and senior Tommy Curtis was the other starter in the backcourt. The Bruins opener that year was against a good Arkansas team, but The Walton Gang made it look easy, winning 101-79. Next came Maryland. The game was played at Pauley Pavilion, and for most of the night it appeared the Bruins were in control. They had a 65-57 lead with minutes left, but the Terps suddenly rallied to bring it to 65-64. Maryland's John Lucas had the ball with the chance to win it, but Meyers blocked his final shot to stave off defeat. But it was close.

After another victory, the Bruins traveled to St Louis for a neutral court encounter with NC State. At first it looked like anyone's game. But when Walton had to sit with foul trouble, the Wolfpack started coming back. They tied the game at 54, but Walton's return soon after sparked the Bruins to a solid 84-66 win. It ended the State winning streak and once again established the Bruins as the team to beat.

Despite signs that the team could be beaten, the Bruins won their first 13 games to run the win streak to a phenomenal 88 games. That's when they traveled to South Bend to meet another unbeaten team, Digger Phelps' Fighting Irish quintet. It had been Notre Dame that ended another Bruin win streak several years earlier. Could they do it again? For most of the game it seemed they couldn't. With Walton leading the way, the Bruins had a comfortable 70-59 lead with just three minutes left in the game. Little did anyone know that they would not score again. The Irish began coming on. Led by Adrian Dantley and John Shumate, Notre Dame reeled off 12 unanswered points to win the game 71-70. The longest winning streak in college basketball history had been ended.

Perhaps the defeat disoriented Walton and company. Four games later they were beaten by Oregon State 61-57, and in their very next encounter they lost to a rather mediocre Oregon team 56-51. It was a new experience for the Bruins. They were actually in a slump. But after that

they resumed their winning ways. Maybe the slump was the best thing for them. Now they had regrouped in time to defend their NCAA title.

But they looked something less than invincible in the first game of the West Regional that year, needing three overtimes to conquer Dayton 111-100. Then they bounced back against San Francisco, winning handily and finding their way into the Final Four one more time. But in the semi-finals they would have a rematch with North Carolina State, which had ended the season ranked number one in both polls. State came in anxious to avenge their early-season loss to the Bruins.

The game was an epic battle from start to finish. Both coaches used just seven players, and the game was tied at 35 at the half. The battle continued, Thompson against Walton, plus a lot more. At the end of regulation it was knotted once again, this time at 65. The first overtime resulted in only one basket by each team, but in the second extra session UCLA spurted to a seven-point lead. It looked over. But somehow the Wolfpack dug down for that little extra something and passed the Bruins at the wire 80-77. The UCLA reign was over.

North Carolina State went on to win the title in 1974,

BELOW LEFT: *Bill Walton's speed and quickness often enabled him to get free inside for easy baskets. In the 1973 final against Memphis State, the big guy made 21 of 22 shots from the floor.*

BELOW RIGHT: *Richard Washington was the UCLA hero in 1975.*

OPPOSITE: *The jumpshooting form of David Thompson. On offense, Thompson could do it all, hitting from the outside or going hard to the hoop.*

defeating Marquette in the championship game 76-64, but in the eyes of most observers the real title game was the semi-final. Walton had finished with 29 points and 18 rebounds, while David Thompson had 28 points and 10 boards. Both superstars had played up to expectations. Years later, Bill Walton was still looking back at that season, still believing his Bruins shouldn't have been stopped. "We played poorly the last two months of that season," he said. "After the win streak was broken we lost four games we should have won. In fact, we should have won 105 in a row. NC State had great talent and a gamebreaker in David Thompson, but we had a seven point lead in overtime and made turnovers. We were not as good a team in a slow-down game. Their four corners slowdown really took us out of it, and I missed a lot of shots around the basket down the stretch."

Bill Walton played during a turbulent time and often espoused a variety of social causes. He was something of an enigma as a superstar and went on to a sometimes great, but sometimes controversial, pro career. But he was the leader of the Walton Gang, one of the greatest college basketball teams of all time.

So Walton, Wilkes, Lee and several others were gone. Now the team would surely go in an eclipse, right? Wrong. Somehow, Wooden found four new starters to go with the returning Dave Meyers, and the Bruins began winning again. With Marques Johnson, Richard Washington, Andre McCarter and Pete Trgovich joining Meyers, the club won its first 12, but suffered several defeats in the second half. They were not favorites when the NCAA's began.

Yet the Bruins won the West Regional and made it once again to the Final Four. In the semi-finals UCLA met Denny Crum's Louisville Cardinals. It was another barnburner. Louisville led by four, with just 48 seconds left, but the Bruins tied it on a pair of free throws by Washington and a hoop by Johnson. In the overtime the Cardinals again led, this time by one in the closing seconds. But Washington hit a baseline jumper at the buzzer to give the Bruins a 75-74 victory.

They almost seemed like a team of destiny, a team playing for all the great ones of the past as well as for themselves. In the finals against a Joe B Hall Kentucky team, the Bruins again took it to the wire. And despite the presence of several outstanding Kentucky players, such as Kevin Grevey and Jack Givens, the Bruins pulled it off, winning 92-85 behind MVP Washington's 28 points. It was the record-setting tenth NCAA title for John Wooden, a record that will probably never be beaten. And with perhaps his most surprising win all sewed up, the Wizard of Westwood announced his retirement.

No team has ever been able to dominate the NCAAs the way UCLA did in the 1960s and 1970s. Surprisingly, one of the few men who says it could happen again is John Wooden. He believes that winning breeds winning and that more good players will come to a winning program. He may be right, but with all the good teams and outstanding players in the game today, it's hard to see one school ever dominating the Final Four the way the Bruins — and the Wizard of Westwood — once did.

TOP RIGHT: *It's Marquette on offense here in the 1974 NCAA title game, but it was North Carolina State that won it by a 76-64 score.*

BOTTOM RIGHT: *UCLA's John Wooden always seemed relaxed, no matter how tense the game.*

OPPOSITE: *Forward Marques Johnson was another fine, all-American player at UCLA during the John Wooden era. The 6-7 Johnson helped the Bruins to their last title in 1975.*

BIGGER AND BETTER THAN EVER

There *was* basketball life after UCLA, though it might have been difficult to convince some people of that during the decade of 1965-75. Still, there had been many other outstanding players on the scene during that time, and a number of outstanding teams. It's just that the Bruins usually seemed to have a little extra magic come NCAA tournament time.

David Thompson and his North Carolina State teams of 1973 and 1974 certainly approached greatness. Besides being the only club to dethrone the Walton Gang, the team was a fine one in its own right. And some of the other players of that period, cagers like Pete Maravich, Bob Lanier, Artis Gilmore, Bob McAdoo and Adrian Dantley, were all great in their own right and proved it all over again in the pros. They just weren't fortunate enough to play on teams that had the overall balance and depth of UCLA.

Besides Alcindor and Walton, Bruins players from the Wooden years appearing on the all-American rosters included Hazzard, Goodrich, Allen, Wicks, Bibby, Wilkes and Meyers. And some of the others weren't far behind. But after Wooden's retirement in 1975 the Bruins would never regain the lofty position they had held for so long. Now the NCAA race would be wide open as more and more teams would contend for the national title.

LEFT: *Though just 6-5, Notre Dame's Adrian Dantley was always a tough inside player. He surprised a lot of college fans and would surprise a lot more with his toughness as a pro.*

ABOVE: *Marques Johnson.*

OPPOSITE ABOVE: *Tough and often controversial, coach Bobby Knight is still a winner who knows how to blend his players into a smooth unit.*

OPPOSITE RIGHT: *Indiana point guard Quinn Buckner takes a jump shot as center Kent Benson (54) gets ready for a rebound. The Hoosiers won over Michigan, 86-68 to take the national championship in 1976.*

The NCAA tournament had expanded to 32 teams in 1975 and would expand again. So there were even more schools with a chance to win, and the expanded field gave more clubs the incentive to play hard right through the end of the season, hoping to get a bid to the tournament and participate in the Final Four. By now the "Final Four" had become a byword for the tourney, with the same kind of significance as the World Series, the Super Bowl or the Stanley Cup. It had become one of the sports biggests spectacles, with all the pomp and pagentry that goes along with events of that magnitude.

It wasn't long before a new favorite was established. Flamboyant Bobby Knight was building a strong team out in Indiana, a team many had thought might go all the way a year earlier. The Hoosiers had won their first 28 games in 1975, but then star forward Scott May broke his arm. Though May continued to play with a cast, he wasn't quite the same player, and it hurt the team. Still, they made it all the way to the Mideast Regional finals, a step away from the Final Four. There, they met Joe B Hall's Kentucky team, a ballclub they had beaten earlier in the season 98-74. But with May hampered by the broken arm, Kentucky upset Indiana 92-90, and Knight's quest for a first national title ended. Yet a year later the Hoosiers were back and better than ever.

May was back in all-American form and was joined by Tom Abernethy at the other forward. Rugged six-foot, nine-inch Kent Benson was a horse in the middle, while lanky Bobby Wilkerson and Quinn Buckner were an able-bodied backcourt combination. Knight's bench was filled with role-players who knew just what they were expected to do when they got into the game. With this combination the Hoosiers rolled through their 1976 regular-season schedule unbeaten and were installed as favorites when the NCAA tourney began.

Knight's team showed its power in a Mideast Regional game against St John's, winning by a 90-70 count as May tallied 33 and Benson 20. Alabama fell next, with May getting 25 points and 16 rebounds. In the regional championships Indiana topped Marquette 65-56 to get into the Final Four. Waiting for them there was the ghost of championships past. UCLA, led by Marques Johnson and Richard Washington, had come on late in the season and had once against won the West. New coach Gene Bartow wanted to show everyone that the Bruins could win without Wooden.

As part of the nation's Bi-Centennial celebration the Final Four was held in historic Philadelphia, at the Spectrum. Michigan was the first team in the finals, whipping surprising Rutgers 86-70, and then the Hoosiers took the court against the Bruins. This time Knight had the unbeaten team, but the Bruins . . . well, they were the Bruins. And even though Indiana had beaten them by 20 points early in the regular season, there were many who thought the

ABOVE: *Richard Washington (31) again tried to play UCLA into the NCAA finals in 1976. Washington, jump shooting here against Notre Dame, helped his team into the semi-finals. But there the Bruins faltered, losing to Indiana 65-51.*

OPPOSITE: *Rutgers (in red and white uniforms) was a Cinderella team in the 1976 tournament. The Scarlet Knights amazed basketball by going undefeated in the regular season. But in the NCAA semi-finals against Michigan, the little team with the big heart lost to Michigan by 16.*

RIGHT: *At 6-9, Kent Benson wasn't a huge center by any standards. But Benson fit into Bobby Knight's game plan and did a great job for the 1976 Indiana national champions.*

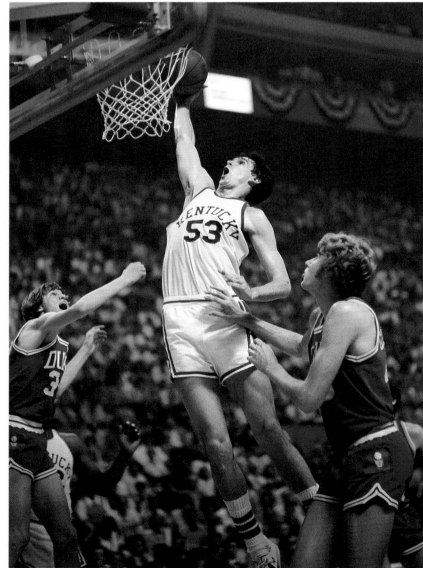

UCLA magic might work once more.

But this time Indiana took control of the game immediately, deploying a balanced attack and a tough defense. It wasn't a high scoring game, but it showed which team was better balanced and stronger. The Hoosiers won 65-51, to enter the finals.

In the finals Indiana's power was evident once again. Michigan had a solid club but couldn't really keep pace with its Big Ten rival. The Hoosiers led 35-29 at the half, then really turned it on to win going away 86-68. May, with 26, and Benson, with 25, led the way. Benson was named tournament MVP.

After that the tournament began to really open up. Marquette, led by guard Butch Lee, upset North Carolina to win it in 1977, with their coach, Al McGuire, weeping openly on the bench in the closing minutes as he climaxed a long coaching career with a national championship. The next year, 1978, it was Kentucky riding home on the shooting of Jack Givens, who exploded for 41 points to lead the Wildcats past a balanced Duke team led by Gene Banks, Mike Gminski and Jim Spanarkel.

Many of the top players were in the NCAA finals during those years. But other familiar names highlighting the college basketball scene were Otis Birdsong of Houston, Bernard King of Tennessee, David Greenwood of UCLA, Phil Ford of North Carolina, Mychan Thompson of Minnesota and a player from unknown Indiana State University, Larry Bird.

OPPOSITE TOP LEFT: *David Greenwood (34) of UCLA and Kent Benson (54) of Indiana battle underneath during 1976 NCAA semifinal action.*

OPPOSITE TOP RIGHT *Joyous Marquette players cut down net after 1977 title win over North Carolina.*

OPPOSITE BOTTOM LEFT: *Playmaker Phil Ford was an all-American for North Carolina in 1977.*

OPPOSITE BOTTOM RIGHT: *Burly Rick Robey (53) helped Kentucky to yet another national title in 1978.*

TOP RIGHT: *Dynamic Al McGuire coached Marquette to a title in 1977, then wept openly on the bench.*

RIGHT: *Indiana's Scott May in action during the 1976 finals with Michigan. May was an all-American college player who was never quite able to repeat his success in the pros. But the Hoosiers wouldn't have won the national title without his help.*

Before the 1978-79 season ended basketball fans all over the country would know about Larry Bird. And they would also know another player whose name would be not only linked with Bird's during a great college season but for years to come in the pros. He was a dynamic Michigan State sophomore named Earvin Johnson. But few people called him Earvin. He was known universally then, as he is now, as Magic.

Larry Bird was born in the small town of French Lick, Indiana. He didn't have an easy childhood, as his family had to work hard to survive. But young Larry took to basketball early, following his older brothers to the courts and struggling to push the ball up into the basket. Pretty soon he was practicing in his room with a rubber ball and bottomless coffee can.

Indiana was always a hotbed for basketball, and young Larry Bird learned to play a team game with a lot of movement and passing. And this concept continued right into his high school years. "The coaches were constantly drilling us on executing the right way, backdoors, pick and rolls, using the backboard on layups," Larry recalled in later years. "They kept banging the fundamentals of the game into us. Make a mistake and you did it over. That was fine with me. I never wanted to leave the court until I got things exactly right. My dream, even then, was to become a pro."

By the time he was a high school senior Larry had grown to a bona fide six feet, nine inches and was being recruited by a number of major colleges. In the fall of 1974 Larry went to Indiana, where he would have played under Bobby Knight. But he just didn't like the feel of the large school and soon left. After an unsettled period in his life he returned to school at Indiana State, which was about a third of the size of Indiana and not particularly known for its bas-

ABOVE: *The amazing Larry Bird singlehandedly made tiny Indiana State a major basketball power in 1979. At 6-9, Bird could do it all, and he took the Sycamores through an unbeaten season and into the finals.*

OPPOSITE: *The other great player of 1979 was soph Earvin "Magic" Johnson of Michigan State. Johnson was a point guard who could do everything and led the Spartans to the NCAA title.*

ketball program. But once Larry Bird got there he immediately began to carry the Sycamores on the strength of his immense basketball talents.

Earvin Johnson was also a local kid who stayed home. Born and raised in East Lansing, Michigan, Earvin was one of ten children. Both his parents worked very hard to support their family. Young Earvin began playing ball with his brothers, much like Larry Bird. Because he was the youngest he had to learn to dribble well just to survive with the bigger kids. He also watched many games on television, and his father was often close at hand. "My father would point out things like a big guard taking a smaller guard underneath," Magic said, "or guys running a pick and roll. By the time I started playing organized ball, whenever the coach asked if anybody knew how to do a three-man weave or a left-handed layup I was always the first one up."

Already an all-star at Everett High School, Magic was also recruited heavily, but he ended up following his good friend Jay Vincent to Michigan State. With freshmen now able to play varsity ball, Magic was a starter in his first season, 1977-78. And, like Bird, it didn't take him long to get some rave notices. "He's most exciting player I've ever seen," said Joe Axelson, the general manager of the NBA Kansas City Kings. "I can't believe that God created a six-foot, eight-inch man who can handle the ball like that."

As for Bird, he had singlehandedly made Indiana State a power to be reckoned with and following his junior year of 1977-78 and was named a first team all-American. Since he had redshirted a year he was also eligible for the NBA draft, and while he had indicated his desire to return to Indiana State for his senior year, Red Auerbach, the wily general manager of the Boston Celtics, drafted him anyway. Always a shrewd judge of talent, Auerbach wasn't about to let the Birdman get away, even if he had to wait another whole year for him.

That set up the 1979 confrontation between Indiana State and Michigan for the NCAA title, Bird against Johnson. During the regular season Bird had averaged 29 points, 15 rebounds and nearly six assists a game as the Sycamores went unbeaten and were ranked number one in the country. Yet critics said they had an easy schedule and were a one-man gang. They all felt they had something to prove.

Michigan State had a slightly different road to take. The Spartans lost center Jay Vincent to injury and stumbled in the early going. After 11 games they were only 6-5 and very mediocre. But Magic and forward Greg Kelser began putting things together, and the Spartans started winning. They won 15 of their final 16 games to finish at 21-6, cracking the top ten at the same time. But the Spartans, too, knew the expanded 40-team NCAA tournament wouldn't be easy.

Bird was coming into the tourney under a handicap. The Sycamores had to win the Missouri Valley tourney to qualify for the big one, and in the final game Larry broke his left thumb. But he quickly decided to continue playing with the thumb wrapped. And the way he played you'd never know he was hurt.

With Bird continuing to perform well and getting help from quality guard Carl Nicks, the Sycamores started out on their final quest. In the Midwest Regional semi-final they topped a tough Oklahoma team 93-72, with Bird tallying 29 points and adding five assists. Now they had to meet Arkansas, a team featuring an outstanding all-American in six-foot, five-inch Sidney Moncrief.

With Bird scoring 25 points in the first 27 minutes, Indiana State took a solid lead. But then Razorback coach Eddie Sutton decided to put the cat-quick Moncrief on Bird, with orders to deny him the ball. The strategy worked, and Arkansas rallied to tie the game at 71, with less than two

BELOW: *Magic Johnson was at his magical best in the 1979 NCAA semi-finals against Pennsylvania. He and his teammate, Greg Kelser, led the Spartans over the Quakers 101-67.*

OPPOSITE: *Larry Bird of Indiana State dribbling with his left hand. Unlike the big men of earlier days, Bird handled the ball like a guard and could shoot both close in and from far out.*

ABOVE: In the title game of 1979 Michigan's State's Greg Kelser was tough underneath, often scoring off nifty passes from Magic. Here Kelser soars for two as Larry Bird seems to be trying to shout the ball out of the basket.

LEFT: *A player who goes all out every game, Larry Bird shows his intensity against West Texas State. He was so good as a junior that Boston Celtic Red Auerbach drafted him as a future.*

OPPOSITE: *The Magic man ready to go into his act. Though just a sophomore in 1979, he had already reached the apex of his game. After the Spartans won the national championship, Magic decided to turn pro.*

minutes left. But after a Razorback turnover the Sycamores had a final chance. Everyone thought Bird would get the ball, but it didn't work that way. A sub forward named Bob Heaton got the final shot . . . and made it. Indiana State won 73-71, and they were on their way to Salt Lake City for the Final Four.

Meanwhile, Magic and Michigan State were also following a similar road. They whipped Louisiana State in the Midwest Regional semifinals 87-71, with Magic scoring 24 points and picking up 12 assists. Then there was a showdown game with Notre Dame, and though just a sopho-

more, Magic Johnson felt this had to be the year. "I don't think the team will be back next year," he said. "Kelser is a senior, and as for me, I don't know what I'm going to do about the pros. So this is it. This is our chance right here."

Once again Johnson and Kelser were great. At one point the thin forward scored seven straight hoops, and four of them came off perfect passes from Magic. When the smoke cleared, Kelser had 34 points, Johnson 13 assists and the Spartans were off to the Final Four with an 80-68 victory.

In the semi-finals Michigan State had it soft. They met a surprising University of Pennsylvania team that simply

didn't have the firepower to compete with them. The Spartans embarrassed the Quakers in the first half, rolling to a 50-17 lead en route to a 101-67 victory.

By contrast, the Sycamores had it hard. They had to play a tough De Paul team. George Mikan's alma mater was still coached by Ray Meyer, and the old man was looking for his first national championship. To many, the Blue Demons were the sentimental favorites. But sentiment could go only so far against Larry Bird. Still nursing the bad thumb, the Birdman put on another super show. The lead changed hands many times in a close ballgame, and but for the shooting of Larry Bird, the Blue Demons would have been on the way to the finals. With five minutes left a Gary Garland hoop gave De Paul a 73-71 lead. The Blue Demons then tried a stall, but it backfired. They had a 74-73 lead when Bob Heaton again hit a key hoop to put the Sycamores in front. After De Paul freshman Mark Aguirre missed a jumper, a final Indiana State free throw iced the game at 76-74. Bird had scored 35 points on 16 of 19 shooting from the floor, and he added 16 rebounds. He had made believers out of everyone.

Everyone, that is, but Michigan State. In the finals, the Spartans used a trapping zone to harass Bird, while Magic and Greg Kelser again played in perfect harmony on offense. Their aggressive defense sent the Sycamores to the line 22 times, but they could convert only 10, and that hurt. The Spartans took a 37-28 halftime lead and hung on to win 75-64, as guard Terry Donnelly sewed it up by hitting five long jumpers when Indiana State looked to be making a run.

Magic Johnson, who had 24 points and seven rebounds, earned MVP honors. Satisfied that his team had done it, Johnson turned pro after his sophomore year. Bird joined the Celtics, quickly justifying Auerbach's year-long wait. And with Magic joining Kareem Abdul Jabbar and the Los Angeles Lakers, the two former college rivals quickly resumed their contests in the pros. But the script had already been written at the Final Four.

Into the 1980s both new and old teams dominated the college scene. The University of Louisville, led by guard Darrell Griffith and forward Rodney McCray, emerged as national champions, defeating a surprising UCLA team in the finals 59-54. Louisville coach Denny Crum had been a longtime assistant to John Wooden, who was on hand to congratulate his protege. Larry Brown had taken over at the helm of the Bruin machine. His club had just 17 wins in the regular season but peaked for the playoffs, defeating Ray Meyer's number one-ranked De Paul team in the semifinals. But in the end it was Louisville.

OPPOSITE: *Magic Johnson (33) and Greg Kelser (32) were double trouble for their rivals all year. They played in perfect harmoney right up until the title game.*

LEFT: *The much-traveled Larry Brown was coaching UCLA in 1980, and his Bruins surprised everyone by reaching the NCAA final before losing to Denny Crum's Louisville Cardinals.*

ABOVE: *Indiana's Landon Turner goes up for a pair in the 1981 title game, as Bobby Knight's Hoosiers win the crown 63-50 over a tough North Carolina.*

LEFT: *Durand "Rudy" Macklin led the Tigers of Louisiana State to the Final Four in 1981.*

BOTTOM LEFT: *Two ace college players meet underneath as North Carolina's Sam Perkins (41) drives on Virginia's 7-4 Ralph Sampson.*

OPPOSITE TOP LEFT: *Isiah Thomas of Indiana scored 23 points from his guard spot in the Hoosier's title win over NC in 1981.*

OPPOSITE TOP RIGHT: *Forward James Worthy was a mainstay in North Carolina's attack.*

OPPOSITE BOTTOM RIGHT: *Seven-foot Sam Bowie of Kentucky was one of the top centers in the college ranks in the early 1980s.*

OPPOSITE BOTTOM LEFT: *In 1982, freshman Michael Jordan was one of the stars of North Carolina's NCAA title team.*

A year later, in 1981, two old hands were back. Bobby Knight and his Indiana Hoosiers met up with Dean Smith's North Carolina Tar Heels. The result was another national title for Indiana, as the Hoosiers won easily, 63-50, breaking the game open in the second half.

But perhaps a bigger story in 1980-81 was the number of outstanding individual players who were now on the college basketball scene. Indiana had a superstar guard in Isaiah Thomas, while North Carolina had a powerful front line with Al Wood, James Worthy and Sam Perkins: All would be future number one draft choices in the NBA. And that wasn't all. The University of Virginia had a seven-foot, four-inch center named Ralph Sampson, who had the Cavaliers ranked number one for a good part of the year: Sampson would be player of the year, but he just didn't have the surrounding cast to go all the way. Brigham Young guard Danny Ainge was another All-American, while DePaul still had Aguirre and Terry Cummings and LSU featured all-American forward Rudy Macklin. Utah boasted a pair of stars, Tom Chambers and Danny Vranes, while Wichita State featured forward Antoine Carr and Cliff Levingston. Other all-Americans included Steve Johnson of Oregon State, Sam Bowie of Kentucky and Kelly Tripucka of Notre Dame.

And the great players continued to come. The 1981-82 season brought another heralded freshman center onto the scene. He was seven-foot Patrick Ewing, who, after a wild recruiting scramble, decided to attend Georgetown University in Washington, DC. The Hoyas, under Coach John Thompson, had a number of other fine ballplayers, including a potential all-American guard named Eric "Sleepy" Floyd. And with competition becoming more intense in the Big East Conference, the Hoyas, with Ewing, were expected to become a national power.

But there were other teams to contend with. North Caro-

lina had added a super freshman guard named Michael Jordan to an already potent lineup that still included big men Worthy and Perkins. The Tar Heels would be the top-ranked team in the country for most of the season. Virginia still had Sampson, and the University of Houston was also building a powerhouse with the likes of Clyde Drexler, Larry Micheaux and a young seven foot center from Nigeria named Akeem Olajuwon.

The Final Four in 1982 would be held at the huge Superdome in New Orleans, a football stadium with a capacity for more than 60,000 fans to watch basketball. That helped make the tournament an even bigger attraction, and some say it was the year that the Final Four finally became a sports event equal to that of the Super Bowl or World Series.

North Carolina had some close calls, but made it to the Final Four with a victory over Villanova. Houston got there by whipping Boston College. Louisville, with Rodney McCray and Derek Smith, topped Alabama-Birminghm to travel there for the second time in three years, while Georgetown, sent to the West Regional, rolled over everyone in sight, including fourth-ranked Oregon State, to go to the Superdome.

In the semi-finals, North Carolina whipped Houston and Georgetown topped Louisville to set up the title game. Freshman Ewing showed his stuff early by swatting away North Carolina's first four shots. But each one was ruled goaltending by the officials, and the Tar Heels had an 8-0 lead without putting the ball through the hoop. But then the Hoyas settled down and reclaimed the lead. After that it was nip and tuck for the remainder of the half. Worthy scored 18 points in the first 20 minutes, but Georgetown held a 32-31 advantage.

The lead continued to change hands in the second half. With six minutes left, Carolina went on top 57-56, as Worthy hit a pair of free throws. Minutes later the Tar Heels

LEFT: *Georgetown's seven-foot freshman, Patrick Ewing, confers with coach John Thompson during a time-out. Ewing led the Hoyas all the way to the NCAA finals, where they lost to North Carolina by a single point.*

ABOVE: *Patrick Ewing in action against Louisville in the 1982 NCAA semi-finals. The big freshman could run the court, play solid defense and block shots. He fit right into the Hoyas pressing, punishing defense.*

OPPOSITE: *Center Sam Perkins of North Carolina cradles the ball in the Tar Heels' 1982 semi-final game against Houston. N C whipped the Cougars 68-63, as Perkins scored 25 points and grabbed ten rebounds.*

were up by three, but a Ewing jumper cut it to 61-60. Then, with less than a minute to go, Sleepy Floyd's jump shot gave the Hoyas the lead, 62-61. Now Carolina worked for perhaps the final shot of the game. With 15 seconds left, freshman Jordan got the ball on the left baseline and calmly sank a 15-footer.

Georgetown tried to break right back. Guard Fred Brown dribbled across halfcourt and thought he spotted a teammate alongside him. He passed the ball . . . right into the hands of James Worthy. It was the costliest of errors. Worthy was fouled, but it didn't matter that he missed both shots. Carolina was able to run the clock out and won it 63-62. And seconds later the TV cameras caught Georgetown coach Thompson hugging the disconsolate Brown. It was a moment of high basketball drama, and millions saw it in their homes, while a record-breaking 61,612 fans at the Superdome witnessed it in person.

A year later, in the 1982-83 season, with Akeem Olajuwon becoming a dominant force at center, Houston's "Phi Slamma Jamma" quintet went 27-2 in the regular season and became the favorites to win the title. But it was a true Cinderella team in North Carolina State that took the basketball world by storm. Led by their charismatic, talkative coach, Jim Valvano, the Wolfpack finished the regular season at 20-10. But they still had to face the Atlantic Coast Conference championships, which gave every ACC team a chance.

Somehow, Valvano's team upset both North Carolina and Virginia to take the ACC crown and gain a berth in the tourney. There, close win seemed to follow close win, until this team of relative unknowns made it to the final against mighty Houston. In another cliff-hanger that had everyone on the edge of their seats, NC State won it at the buzzer, when Lorenzo Charles grabbed an air-ball and put it home.

LEFT: *Nigerian-born Akeem Olajuwon came to the University of Houston with little experience in the game and emerged as an all-American and future pro star. The seven-foot player led the Cougars to the 1983 NCAA title game, scored 20 points and grabbed 18 rebounds, but his team lost to North Carolina State 54-52.*

OPPOSITE: *A Patrick Ewing-Akeem Olajuwon matchup was a highly anticipated event. It happened in the 1984 title game in Seattle. While Olajuwon is beating Ewing to the tap here, and outscored his rival 15-10, it was Georgetown that won the national championship 84-75 in a mild upset. Both mighty centers soon became heated rivals in the NBA.*

The all-American roster that year featured Ewing, Jordan, Perkins, Sampson, Wayman Tisdale of Oklahoma and Keith Lee of Memphis State, all exciting, great college players. Then, in 1983-84, the game continued to emphasize its showcase, the NCA tournament, by increasing the field to 54 teams. The Final Four had benefitted by the two great title games and by giving more teams a chance to compete, and interest around the country was heightened even more.

In addition to the competition, the tournament had become a fantastic moneymaker, not only for the NCAA but for the schools as well. Whereas the winning school in the mid-1950s would receive something in the area of $10-12,000, the national champion in the mid-1980s was earning more than $1 million for the university. That, in itself, was an incentive to build a program and go after the title. And the game had also become more and more of a television spectacular. Even before the NCAA tournament began a multitude of college games were shown on regional and national television, especially during the second half of the season, when the various conference races were really heating up. By the time the NCAAs rolled around fans were familiar with many of the teams, as well as the outstanding players.

In the eyes of many, the big man was beginning to really dominate the game again in 1983-84. Georgetown had Patrick Ewing back, and Akeem Olajuwon was getting better and better at Houston. In addition, Joe B Hall at Kentucky had seven-foot Sam Bowie and six-foot, 11-inch Mel Turpin in the lineup at the same time. One of these teams, it was thought, would emerge as number one for the year.

Ewing was by no means a one-man gang at Georgetown. Coach John Thompson — himself a big man at six feet, ten inches — had put together an outstanding team, one that could strike quickly and defend tenaciously. Point guard Michael Jackson worked very well with Ewing, and both were complemented by six-foot, seven-inch freshman Reggie Williams at one forward and tough six-foot, nine-inch

BELOW: *Keith Lee of Memphis State was still another fine big man to emerge in the 1980s. Here the rail-thin Lee (24) grabs a key rebound in a game against Georgetown.*

OPPOSITE: *Georgetown frosh Reggie Williams (34) was a poised and polished performer from the beginning of his college career. In the 1984 title game the 6-7 Williams came off the bench to score 19 big points.*

Michael Graham at the other. David Wingate was the shooting guard, and the team also had great role players. Gene Smith was a defensive specialist, Bill Martin could fill in at either forward slot and guard Fred Brown, who had thrown the errant pass two years before, was also back after missing a year to injury.

Playing in the very tough and competitive Big East Conference, the Hoyas registered a 29-3 mark during the regular season. For some reason they were sent to the West Regional in the tournament, but after a close call with SMU's stalling tactics the Hoyas rolled over Nevada-Las Vegas and Dayton to head for Seattle and the Final Four.

And what they found was a veritable convention of big men. Kentucky, with Bowie and Turpin, arrived via the Mideast and victories over Brigham Young, Louisville and Illinois. Houston and Olajuwon came roaring out of the Midwest, whipping Louisiana Tech, Memphis State and Wake Forest in the process. The only surprise was Virginia. The ACC team no longer had Ralph Sampson, but they nevertheless had squeezed past Iona, Syracuse, Arkansas and Indiana.

In the semi-finals Virginia's stall almost took the Cavaliers to an upset victory over Houston. The game was tied at the end of regulation, but the Cougars managed to pull it out in OT. Then came the second game, and this one has people talking to this day. Kentucky started like a house on fire. Not ony did their Wildcats take a 27-15 lead after just 11 minutes, they already had Georgetown's Ewing on the

bench with three fouls. They seemed totally in command.

Without his big man in the lineup, Coach Thompson went to his next best weapon, the full court press. Georgetown's press was a smothering one, and if a team couldn't break it immediately it was in trouble. Kentucky couldn't break it. With Ewing still on the bench, Georgetown cut the Kentucky lead to 29-22 by the half. Mel Turpin's jumper with three minutes remaining was the only Wildcat score after they had built their initial 27-15 lead.

Then, in the second half, Georgetown came out fast once again, while Kentucky didn't come out at all. In one of the strangest fadeaways in the history of the tournament the Wildcats went stone cold. They failed to score the first 14 times they had the ball in the second half, and they would

go a full ten minutes before getting a hoop. Georgetown would move in front by 34-29 before the Wildcats could score. Then another 11 straight Hoya points made it 45-31. There was little Kentucky could do. The game ended with Georgetown winning 53-40. In the second half a very good Kentucky team had made just three of 33 field goal tries, an NCAA record for futility. In addition, their five starters missed all 21 shots they had taken in the final 20 minutes.

Now the question was whether the Georgetown defense could do the same thing to Houston and their big man, Olajuwon. While the result in the final wasn't quite as devastating, it was nevertheless convincing. Once again the Hoyas had to overcome an early deficit, as the Cougars jumped in front 10-2. But the Hoyas stormed back behind the shooting of David Wingate and Reggie Williams, while Ewing and Michael Graham did the job up front. This time it was Olajuwon who had to sit with foul trouble, and the Hoyas took a 40-30 halftime lead. When Olajuwon got his fourth personal just 23 seconds into the second half, the game was all but over. Though Houston closed to four, and then three at 57-54, they got no closer. The Hoyas' big men took command again, and Georgetown went on to win it 84-75, becoming national champions for the first time. Williams led the way with 19 points, while Patrick Ewing was named tournament MVP.

A year later, Georgetown was back. Ewing was a senior, and the Hoyas were favorites to repeat. But the 1984-85 sea-

son showed the basketball world something else, and that was simply that the Big East Conference had become perhaps the strongest in the country. Besides Georgetown, St John's and Syracuse had outstanding teams, and in the NCAA tournament another Big East team emerged as a real Cinderella ballclub. They were the Wildcats of Villanova. Coached by the dynamic Rollie Massimino, the Wildcats were a slightly better than mediocre 19-10 during the regular season. But they played in the Big East and had a tough schedule, so they received at large bid to the tournament and proceeded to make the most of their unexpected opportunity. When the smoke from the playdowns cleared, there were three Big East teams in the Final Four.

LEFT: *Melvin Turpin, one of Kentucky's "Twin Towers," takes a jumper in first half action against Georgetown in the 1984 NCAA semi-finals. With the 6-11 Turpin and 7-1 Sam Bowie in the lineup, many felt the Wildcats had a chance to defeat the Hoyas. Kentucky led early and still had a seven-point lead at the half. But then the Hoyas took over as the Wildcats went ice cold and lost 53-40.*

OPPOSITE: *The Memphis State Tigers had plenty of power in 1985, including 7-0 William Bedford (50) and 6-10 Keith Lee. They were the only non-Big East team to make the Final Four that year and were favored for beat Villanova in the semi-finals. But things don't always turn out as expected, and Memphis State was beaten 52-45.*

Georgetown was there and the clear favorite to repeat. St John's, with all-Americans Chris Mullin and Walter Berry, had beaten the Hoyas in the regular season and would be meeting them again in the semifinals. In the other semi, Memphis State, with Keith Lee and William Bedford, figured to have an easy time with the other finalist, the Cinderella Wildcats of Villanova. It marked the first time a single conference had sent three teams to the Final Four.

Try as they might, St John's could not match their mid-season victory over Georgetown. The Hoyas looked invincible, winning easily 77-59 behind Reggie Williams' 20 points and Ewing's 16. And in the other semi-final there was a big surprise: Villanova had beaten Memphis State 52-45.

Now the Wildcats would be meeting the Hoyas in an all-Big East final. But very few people gave Massimino's team much of a chance to win. Even Massimino himself didn't sound too confident when he said that his team "must play a perfect game, but even that might not be enough."

But soon after the Wildcats took the floor for the final at the Adolph Rupp Arena in Lexington it became obvious that Georgetown was not going to have an easy time of it. For Villanova was shooting the eyes out of the basket. Harold Pressley, Dwayne McClain, Ed Pinckney, Gary McLain and Harold Jensen got hot and forgot to cool off. With McLain doing a masterful ballhandling job to break the Georgetown press, and the six-foot, nine-inch Pinckney fighting

OPPOSITE: *Ed Pinckney (54) was Villanova's big man. He wasn't a super center, but in the 1985 NCAA tourney, he proved more than equal to the task.*

ABOVE: *Wayman Tisdale (23) of Oklahoma.*

RIGHT: *Player of the Year Chris Mullin (right) of St John's.*

Ewing to a standoff on the boards, Villanova battled to a 29-28 halftime lead. Still, the crowd of 23,124 waited for the collapse. For the Georgetown pressure was unending.

Villanova's shooting in the second half was strictly unbelievable. They took a 36-30 advantage, then worked their way to a 53-48 lead. But at that point the Hoya defensive pressure began taking its toll, and Wildcat turnovers helped Georgetown into their first lead of the second half, 54-53, with four minutes left. Now would they fold?

No way. A Georgetown turnover gave Villanova the ball, and seconds later the Wildcats had the lead once again. Then the hot shooting resumed, and when the smoke cleared, Villanova had won it, 66-64, in one of the great upsets in NCAA history. And to do it, the Wildcats had set a record by shooting 78.6 from the field. In the second half alone they tickled the twine at an incredible 90 percent rate. Harold Jensen had hit five long jumpers in the second half in five tries. Pinckney, with 16 points and six rebounds in the final, was named the MVP. But the team as a whole really deserved the Most Valuable prize, along with their coach, Rollie Massimino, who refused to let his team die.

The Ewing era was finally over. The big guy had helped Georgetown to three finals in four years, and he was now on his way to the pros. Olajuwon had gone the year before, so there would be new big men coming along. Tisdale of Oklahoma, Lee of Memphis State and Mullin of St John's were also on the all-American roster in 1985, along with a speedy guard from Duke named Johnny Dawkins.

With three cliff-hangers in four years, the NCAA excitement continued to grow, and in 1986 the field was expanded once more, this time to 64 teams. Though it seemed at first that the tournament was getting too big and too bulky, fans seem to enjoy seeing more teams in action and having more schools with a chance to win. So there were really no major problems.

Duke, with Johnny Dawkins back, was the top-rated team in the country, compiling a 28-2 record in the regular season. And with Dawkins leading the way, the Blue Devils took four straight tournament games to work their way into the Final Four, this time held in Dallas. Dawkins had games of 27, 25, 25 and 28 as his club whipped Mississippi Valley State, Old Dominion, De Paul and Navy. The presence of the first two clubs reflected the new 64-team field: Smaller schools such as those never would have gotten into the action in the old days.

Meanwhile there was a battle in the other spots, a battle won by Denny Crum's Louisville quintet, led by a seniors Milt Wagner, Jeff Hall and Billy Thompson. Louisville would defeat LSU in one semi-final, while Duke whipped Kansas in the other, with Dawkins having 24 points. It was expected that the speedy guard would lead his team to the championship. But after Villanova's win the year before, there were no sure things.

Denny Crum always had his teams ready. In addition to his seniors he had a six-foot, nine-inch freshman center, aptly nicknamed Pervis "Never Nervous" Ellison, who dominated the game inside and helped keep the Cardinals close in the first half. Though Duke led 37-34 at intermission, it was still a ballgame.

In the second half it stayed close all the way, neither team really able to extend a lead. In the end, it was the play of Ellison that won it. With a little more than four minutes left,

the young center muscled inside to score and give his team a 63-62 lead. With Louisville up 66-65 and 2:40 left, Crum ordered a stall, and the clock ran down to 40 seconds. Jeff Hall took a shot, but it was way off the mark. Suddenly, there was Ellison, grabbing the airball and putting it in the hoop for a 68-65 Louisville advantage. From there the Cardinals hung on to give Crum his second championship, 72-69. Ellison had 25 points and 11 rebounds to take the MVP prize from Dawkins, who finished with 24. The freshman had come through under pressure, showing just why he was called Never Nervous. And once again the tournament had been a huge success.

In the 1986-87 season the college game made another major change. This was the three-point field goal rule, a rule that had come to pro basketball several years earlier. Now, any jumpshot taken beyond 19 feet, six inches was good for three points. The object was to inject more excitement into the sport and to give the little man a more prominent role in the outcome of a ballgame. And while this proved true on several counts, it was still a big man who dominated the game and got more than his share of national headlines.

He was a seven-foot, one-inch center performing in the unlikely setting of the Naval Academy. When David Robinson was accepted at Annapolis he still hadn't grown to his full height. But as he grew and matured it was apparent that he had become a outstanding basketball player, a well-coordinated big man who could score and rebound, run and block shots. The only question was how much time would he have to spend in the Navy before turning pro? He did not have the surrounding cast that most outstanding big men have — the Naval Academy team was not a Georgetown — but Robinson proved enough of a one-man gang to engineer a number of upsets during his final two seasons playing at Annapolis.

OPPOSITE TOP RIGHT: *Duke's cat-quick guard, Johnny Dawkins, was one of the top players in the nation in 1986. He led the Blue Devils to a 32-2 and a spot in the Final Four. The lightning lefty scored 24 points in Duke's 71-67 semi-final victory over Kansas, and while he got 24 more in the final, his team lost to Louisville 72-69.*

OPPOSITE BOTTOM LEFT: *Still carrying his rolled-up program, a habit learned from mentor John Wooden at UCLA, Louisville's Denny Crum coached the Cardinals to a 1986 title.*

RIGHT: *Louisville's frosh center, Pervis "Never Nervous" Ellison, shown in action here against Kentucky, was a star from his first game. By the time the NCAAs rolled around, Ellison was playing like a seasoned pro. He scored 25 points and grabbed 11 rebounds in the final game to lead the Cardinals past Duke.*

As for the three-point shot, well, there were a number of purists who were dead set aganst it, but there were also teams which used it to win ballgames. In a sense, it was a geat equalizer, the little man's answer to the slam dunk. And as it turned out, two of the Final Four teams made major use of the three-point shot.

The two were Providence, another Big East club and a true Cinderella team under Coach Rick Patino, a team without a superstar, but a club that could bury the jumper from deep. The other was Jerry Tarkanian's Nevada-Las Vegas team, that had guard Freddie Banks firing three-pointers while rugged Armon Gilliam did the job underneath. In fact, a third Final Four team, Bobby Knight's Indiana Hoosiers, also had a potent three-point threat in all-American guard Steve Alford. Only Syracuse, from the Big East, wasn't really a threat to hit from way out.

So in less than a year, the three-point shot had become an integral part of the college game, and appeared to have arrived for good. It would be showcased in the finals, played at the New Orleans Superdome before nearly 65,000 screaming fans.

The two Big East teams met in the first semi-final, and Syracuse pretty much dominated the action from the outset, keeping Patino's sharpshooters from drilling deep and winning by a score of 77-63. The second game was a shootout. Indiana finally won it 97-93, but not before UNLV's Banks scored 38, including a brace of three-pointers, and Armon Gilliam added 32. But the Hoosiers answered with 33 from Alford and good balance from the other starters to pull the game out.

Once again the final was a nail-biter. Syracuse used its big man, Rony Seikaly, to get the lead in the early going, but Indiana came right back behind Alford, who decided early on that he was going to shoot three-pointers whenever he had the chance. At the half the Hoosiers led by one, 34-33, and the game stayed close all the way. Strangely enough, only four of the Hoosiers scored, but three of them (Alford, Daryl Thomas and Keith Smart) had 20 or more points. But with the game up for grabs, no one really cared who got the points.

Once again the game went to the final seconds. Syracuse had taken the lead 74-73, but Indiana had the last shot, and Keith Smart hit it from the left baseline to give the Hoosiers a dramatic 74-73 victory and Bobby Knight his third national championship. Steve Alford had also shown everyone just what the three-point rule could do. He hit seven of his ten three-point attempts, and while he finished with just eight field goals, he had 23 points. Syracuse, as a team, made just four of ten from three-point range, so you could accurately say that the home run ball was the difference.

After the game, Knight said that he didn't think his team could be considered a great one, but then he added: "What this team had was a great quality in its ability to play well in crucial situations and get the key points. They did it all through the tournament."

And perhaps that is the best way to describe today's game

OPPOSITE FAR LEFT: *Bobby Knight, urging his Indiana Hoosiers to their third national crown. The Hoosiers stopped Syracuse 74-73.*

OPPOSITE LEFT: *1987 was the first year of the three-point field goal, and in the NCAA final Indiana's Steve Alford got seven of them.*

ABOVE: *Indiana guard Keith Smart shooting over the Syracuse defense in the NCAA title game. Smart had 21 points, including a clutch jumper in the final seconds that gave the Hoosiers their one-point victory.*

of college basketball. The sport has a great quality, and that quality seems to show best in crucial situations, especially in the NCAA Tournament, the game's showcase. As the sport heads toward the twenty-first century there is no sign that it's going to slow down or stop growing. Some of today's great college players will go on into the pros; the majority will simply leave big-time athletics behind them. But whatever they do, they will always have their memories of their experiences on the court, playing a game that was started long ago for casual recreation and that became one of the greatest in the world. To say that they — and we — owe a debt to James Naismith understates the case.

129

Chris Leonard, of the Original Celtics had the look of a professional basketball player of the 1920s. The Celtics were pro basketball's first great dynasty.

PART 3

The Pro Game

PIONEERS

Professional basketball didn't appear overnight. Sure, there were teams in the early days, and a number of leagues as well. But they were all over the place, each with its own set of rules and each playing in different types of buildings. And most early attempts to organize the sport and bring it to a par with baseball and football ended in failure. In fact, the pro game did not become firmly established until the late 1940s and early 1950s. Until then it was often a very different game from what it is today, with variations in rules in each part of the country.

For example, a fan watching a professional basketball game in 1920 might very well have been sitting in a high school gymnasium, or even at a local dance hall where there was often more interest in the dancing at halftime and afterward than in the game itself. On a few occasions the game was even played in basements — indeed, it was played anyplace where a couple of baskets could be erected and some lines could be put down to mark the court, the dimensions of which were usually dictated by the amount of space available.

In some places the early pro basketball fan might find a wire cage erected around the court, a device used to keep the ball and the players in play. Many a player was cut or injured by being pushed into the various kinds of cages. Other courts were surrounded by a flexible net, which the players could bounce off, similar to the way a fighter comes off the ropes around a boxing ring. And in still other places there were open courts similar to those of today. Each game was played differently, and the players had to be ready to adjust instantly to the particular exigencies of the cage, net or open court. In that respect the early college game was much more standardized.

And that wasn't the only inconsistency in the early days of the pro game. Some courts used the backboard, others didn't, the hoop simply coming out over the court via a long pipe. Where there were backboards, they often differed, some being wood, others glass and still others wire. Playing conditions varied from place to place and from league to league. While baseball's Major Leagues, the National Football League, and the National Hockey League were pretty much permanently established by the mid-1920s, there was no similar organization in basketball. Leagues came and went with monotonous regularity.

Most professional leagues in the early days operated only on weekends, making some professional players part-time athletes. Those who wanted to play full-time had to be in two or more leagues at once, playing for more than one team and picking up games and a few dollars wherever and whenever they could. Some of the best teams of those early years, such as the Original Celtics and the New York Renaissance, were great barnstorming teams, going anywhere to play if the guaranteed pay was enough. Barnstorming was one of the few ways players could be fulltime pros back then.

OPPOSITE: *The Newton Eagles, a pro team whose players belonged to Company D of the Kansas National Guard in 1902. The Eagles learned the game from pioneer W C "Will" Kosa, who also established the first organized group of teams in the area. Top row, left to right, are Howard Randall, Guy Sawyer, and Chris Hayman. Seated, l to r, John Landers; John Hetzel, coach-manager; and Archie Caveney.*

RIGHT: *In 1921 the pro game was still in its infancy, and basketball was still virtually unknown to many potential players. So there was still much instruction needed. Here, two YMCA players demonstrate a very obvious foul. Once again, note the old fashioned, seamed and unsatisfactory ball.*

There was also a complete lack of consistency in the early rules. In one league a player might find the old two-hand dribble, where he could dribble, stop, then dribble again, tantamount to a double dribble violation today. But not everyone played that way. The colleges, for instance, already had the one-hand dribble, as did some of the pro leagues. Each team had house rules of one kind or another. This made it especially difficult for college players to adjust to the pro game in the 1920s and early 1930s, so many of them gave up the sport as soon as their college days were over.

Those who played pro ball then lived a singularly different kind of life. The schedule was often unpredictable and travel was very difficult. In the early days the players rarely traveled as a team. It was their responsibility to get to the game, whether it be by car, by train, by trolley or even by ferry boat. The barnstorming teams often had to travel long distances in a short time, and since basketball has always been a winter sport, the players were much at the mercy of the weather. In addition, accommodations were often uncertain. There were no luxury motels then. Rather, the players stayed in old hotels or worse, and they never knew ahead of time if they would have a soft bed, a hot shower or a decent meal. Sometimes they found the best thing was camp in the gymnasium until game time.

These basic conditions persisted right into the 1930s, and to an extent into the early 1940s. College basketball grew

ABOVE: *This tough-looking bunch of old pro ballplayers were known as the Crescents, and they defeated many of the top college teams in New York City in 1920, winning 23 of their 25 games.*

OPPOSITE: *Hall of Famer Benny Borgmann played in some 2500 pro games in many different early leagues, beginning before 1920. He was a top scorer when, as now, scorers were always in demand.*

more rapidly than the pro game, and when the rules were finally more or less standardized in the 1930s it was the pros who gave up such long-standing traditions as the two-handed dribble, as well as the cage and net games, to accommodate the colleges and to try to induce more college players to continue with basketball as professionals.

In spite of the changes, the problem of trying to create a stable professional league remained unsolved. Numerous attempts were made in the late 1920s, throughout the 1930s and into the early 1940s. None of them worked. In some cases there weren't enough available arenas, in others the leagues just weren't balanced, the quality of the product not good enough to develop and sustain fan interest. It wasn't until after World War II, when the National Basketball League and the Basketball Association of America merged to form what ultimately became the National Basketball Association, that the game finally became the big-time sport that the pioneer players had wanted for so long.

Professional basketball began about the same time as the college game. Obviously not all the young men who started playing the sport at the YMCAs in the 1890s went to college. Many of them wanted to continue playing, and when they would no longer play at the "Y" they began looking elsewhere. Ultimately, this often meant renting places for their games. And to earn back the rent money, the players began charging admission. Any money over and above the rent they would split among themselves. They were, in effect, professionals.

By 1898 this loose network of professional players saw the formation of the first real league. It was supposedly started by a man named William Scheffer and called the National Basketball League, though there was very little that was "national" about it. All the teams were from the Philadelphia area, with several New York teams eventually added. The league hung on until 1903, when it was disbanded. When another league, the Philadelphia League, sprang up soon thereafter the pattern was set. Leagues would be formed and just as suddenly disbanded.

One of the more stable early leagues was the Eastern League, which was started in 1910 and lasted until 1922. The original teams were from Princeton, Trenton, Germantown, Reading, Jasper, DeNeri and Elizabeth. Some great early players, such as Johnny Beckman and Nat Holman, played in the Eastern League, Beckman at Reading and Holman with Germantown. And in the league's final season, 1922, the team that won the championship was the New York Celtics, the name most synonymous with the early days of the professional game.

OPPOSITE: *Elmer Ripley during his coaching days. Ripley began playing pro ball in Carbondale, Pa, and later played for the Original Celtics.*

BELOW: *The Buffalo Germans, a turn-of-the-century pro team shown in 1902. Actually, the Germans started as a teenage team and didn't turn pro until 1904. They once won 111 straight games, and disbanded in 1926.*

RIGHT: *This is Lou Wachter of the Troy Trojans, an upstate New York pro team organized by Lou's brother, Ed. Ed Wachter started the team to challenge the Buffalo Germans. It's said the Trojans were pro ball's first, fast-breaking team and besides the Wachter brothers had such early stars as Chief Muller and Jack Inglis. Lou Wachter later coached at Dartmouth.*

LEFT: *This is the legendary Nat Holman during his days with the Original Celtics. Holman was one of the most competitive players of his day. He often took a beating from bigger and stronger players but never quit. He began coaching City College during his playing days, coaching for 37 years beginning in 1920. Holman has been a part of the pro game since its infancy and has seen it grow into a major sport. He is a member of Basketball's Hall of Fame.*

OPPOSITE RIGHT: *Like many of the early pro players, Barney Sedran wasn't a big man, standing just 5-4. Born in 1891, Sedran was a top player from 1911 to 1926, playing with such legendary teams as the New York Whirlwinds. He often teamed with another little man, Marty Friedman, and together they were known as the "Heavenly Twins."*

OPPOSITE FAR RIGHT: *Muscular Ed Wachter was the man who started the Troy Trojans and was one of the fine early players in the pro game. Wachter was a center and led the Trojans to titles in both the New York State and Hudson River Leagues.*

One of the pioneer professional players was Elmer Ripley, a member of the Hall of Fame, who was born in New York in 1891, the same year that James Naismith invented the game. Ripley played the professional game right from his teenage years, so his recollections of those days ran deep. A short time before his death, Ripley took time to talk about the various conditions the pros were faced with back then. "One reason there wasn't much dribbling in the early game was the ball. It was made of leather and it used to get out of shape. You had to put a bladder in it and then blow it up. So nobody dribbled. You moved the ball and you moved yourself."

Ripley also spoke about some of the strange playing conditions and rough play of the early pro game, conditions that made it quite different from the much better organized college game. "They used to have a basketball team at every Catholic Church in Brooklyn, and many times they played down the basement with big pillars. The referee would throw the ball up and then get behind one of the pillars so he wouldn't get killed.

"We used to say, 'All friendship ceases, protect yourself at all times'," said Ripley. "But that's the way it went because the fellas loved to play and were often on more than one team at a time."

One reason for the rough play in the early pro game was that no one fouled out. A player could commit ten or 12 fouls and still be in the game. So many of the fouls were pretty obvious and pretty rough. As Nat Holman once said, "Basketball to many players back then meant chopping the opponent down. Fighting was the only reason a player would be removed from a game."

Holman was born in 1896 and thus played in the very early days of the game also. He always played while continuing with his schooling. And after getting a degree in physical education he was hired by City College of New York as a tutor, soccer coach and freshman basketball coach. Yet while he always kept his job at CCNY, Nat Holman managed to play pro basketball as often as he could.

He played for both Germantown in the Eastern League and Scranton in the Penn State League at the same time. The Eastern League games were played in a reinforced wire cage, which made it necessary for the players to wear hip pads, an aluminum cup and elbow and knee guards. Holman also recalled that the Eastern League had backboards with glass on both sides and a wooden piece down the middle, with the hoop 12 inches from the board.

Holman remembered a game played in Carbondale, Pennsylvania, in which the court was surrounded by a high net.

He was playing with Bill Manning's team against a Carbondale team with Elmer Ripley, Andy Swells and Jack Inglis. It was a close game until Inglis pulled a maneuver that Holman would never forget. "Jack started down the left side of the court at top speed with me right on top of him. As we got to the net he jumped up as high as he could and with his left hand grabbed the net, pulled himself up and did a quarter turn right. Swells fired a baseball pass to him, which he caught with one hand against his chest, and with a little flick he tossed it into the open basket. And there I was, helpless, down below looking up at him."

The names of many of the great players from those earliest days are now largely forgotten. Except for those few remaining pioneer players, no one really talks about the exploits of Jack Inglis. Yet he played his sport at the time Babe Ruth played baseball, Red Grange football and Jack Dempsey wowed the boxing world. They are legends. But because basketball was behind the other sports, men like Inglis, Barney Sedran, Marty Friedman, the Wachters, Chuck Passon and their contemporaries were mostly ignored. They cannot fairly be compared with the players of the later eras, not only because of the obvious difference in size but because of the different rules. But the fact that the early pros stuck it out made all that followed possible.

THE ORIGINAL CELTICS

Perhaps the most well-known team name in all of basketball, the Celtics, oddly enough did not originate in Boston. Though the Boston Celtics represent the most successful professional franchise in National Basketball Association history, it was another Celtics team that is widely considered the best of all the early barnstorming teams.

The name was actually first used as far back as 1912, when a man named Frank McCormack put together a team to play the dance hall circuit on New York's west side. The name "Celtics" came from a social club that was part of the Hudson Guild Settlement House in New York. The team played their home games at the Settlement House and often participated in as many as five leagues at once.

By 1916 the team was known as the New York Celtics, and they began playing their games at the Amsterdam Opera House. No one could accuse basketball of charging inflated prices back then. Tickets cost 35 cents for men and 15 cents for women. So the people came, and the Celtics began their great winning tradition.

When Frank McCormack left for the service during World War I he apparently lost control of the team, for when he returned he found the Celtics playing for a man named Jim Furey. Because of a lawsuit brought by McCormack, Furey changed the name from the New York Celtics to the Original Celtics. But he had many of the same players who had performed for McCormack, and their games were eventually played at the 71st Regiment Armory at Park Avenue and 34th Street. With John Whitty as the coach, the Original Celtics began to find outstanding players such as Dutch Dehnert and Johnny Beckman, joining Pete Barry, Joe Tripp, Mike Smolick, Ernie Reich and Eddie White. The Celtics were now hard to beat.

At the same time, the famous promoter Tex Rickard, who was running Madison Square Garden, formed his own team, the Whirlwinds, and packed it with stars like Nat Holman, Chris Leonard, Barney Sedran and Marty Friedman, the latter two being Philadelphia ballplayers nicknamed the Heavenly Twins.

The two great teams remained independent, playing and usually beating any and all comers except one another. Finally, at the end of the 1921 season they met. Playing before a screaming crowd of some 11,000 fans at the Armory, the Whirlwinds won 40-27. But in a rematch, the Celtics were victorious 26-24. With fans clamoring for a rubber match, the promoters waffled. Fearing violence on the part of each team's fanatical fans, they called it off.

That's when Jim Furey put the final stamp of greatness on the Celtics. He talked Nat Holman and Chris Leonard into leaving the Whirlwinds for his club. Later, he added Horse Haggerty, a six-foot, four-inch, 225-pound giant who might have been pro ball's first enforcer, and Davey Banks, who was a great player for the Philadelphia SPHA's. And when a couple of the early players began getting up in years, the team added Nat Hickey and Joe Lapchick. They

OPPOSITE: *The Original Celtics, as they looked in December 1920. They began play in 1912 and continued to play into the early 1930s. But it was in the 1920s that the Celtics dominated the pro game as perhaps its greatest team. In the front row, l to r, Manager Jim Furey, Ernie Reich, Johnny Beckman, Tom Furey. Back row l to r, John Whitty, Dutch Dehnert, Joe Tripp, Pete Barry and Mike Smolnick.*

ABOVE: *Johnny Beckman of the Celtics, who was born in 1895, was sometimes known as the "Babe Ruth of Basketball" for his outstanding play. He began his pro career in 1910 and is a member of the Basketball Hall of Fame.*

RIGHT: *Nat Holman was an outstanding free throw shooter, as well as a great all-around player. In the early days of the pro game, one player often took all of his team's free throws. With the Celtics, that man was Holman.*

were a tough club to beat, from the time they were first organized all the way into the 1930s.

Yet during their barnstorming days, the Celtics played in many different kinds of halls and arenas. Nat Holman recalled playing on a hockey rink in Providence, Rhode Island, where the players banged each other into the boards, much as they would in a hockey game. They also played in dancehalls, where the drinking and dancing at halftime would leave the court a slippery mess in the second half. "For places like this we always wore special shoes with holes in the soles," Holman said. "Then we would put vaseline in the holes so the shoes would stick to the floor. One time, I remember we used kerosene and it ruined the floor."

Like other pro teams of the time, the Celtics didn't play any zone defense. It was strictly a man-to-man game because the players were so skilled that they could beat a zone with set-shooting or with ball movement. It was also a team game, no room for selfishness or individual heroics. If there was an open man, you hit him. But there were no set plays, either. Nat Holman once described the Celtic style as free, open and spontaneous. The team worked its plays around the center jump. There were no real deliniations then between forwards and guards, and one man did the foul shooting for the entire team.

OPPOSITE TOP: *Abe Saperstein and his 1930-31 Harlem Globetrotters, a great early black team that was to become the most entertaining team ever. Standing, l to r, Saperstein, Toots Wright, Byron Long, Inman Jackson and William Oliver. Seated is Al Pullins.*

OPPOSITE BOTTOM: *The Renaissance, organized by Robert L Douglas (inset) was the first great black team. The club won more than 2300 games. Left to right, Clarence "Fat" Jenkins, Bill Yancey, John Holt, James "Pappy" Ricks, Eyre Saitch, Charles "Tarzan" Cooper, and William "Wee Willie" Smith.*

RIGHT: *An early publicity shot of Celtic Henry "Dutch" Dehnert. Dehnert would often take passes at the foul line and pass off to cutting teammates. It was the beginning of the pivot play, and Dehnert was its best proponent in the early days of the pro game.*

The Celtics were a balanced team, with no superstars. They always played with a pivot man, first Dutch Dehnert and later Joe Lapchick. But the pivot man did not shoot a hook shot back then. He usually stayed on the foul line with his back to the basket. When he got the pass other men could cut off him for a return pass. If the defensive man switched, the pivot man would get the ball back for an easy hoop. Much of their offense worked off the pivot, while the man-to-man defense was tough and solid.

So successful were the Celtics that the players soon went from being paid by the game to getting a seasonal salary. Holman recalled getting $10 to $15 a game when he first began playing, then moving up to $25 to $50 a game. And a few top players could bring in as much as $75. When the early leagues began, some of the players began earning in the neighborhood of $4000 to $5000 a season. The Celtics were in the forefront of these seasonal salaries.

Though the team won the majority of its games, it was not totally invincible. One team that challenged the Celtics was the Renaissance Big Five, one of the earliest black pro teams. Organized by Bob Douglas, who managed the Renaissance Casino in New York City's Harlem section, the Renaissance Big Five started in 1922 and quickly became one of the best barnstorming teams ever. While the records of some of the early barnstorming teams are often difficult to verify, it's thought that Douglas and the Rens won around 2300 games, while losing fewer than 400. In 1933 there is a recorded 88-game win streak, with all victories coming on the road.

The Rens really hit their stride in the early 1930s, just as

143

the Celtics were breaking up. In the eyes of many who remember, from about 1932 to 1936 the Renaissance Big Five were the best team in the nation. Records show the team winning 473 and losing just 49 during that span, including a 127-7 record in 1933-34. During each of these years the Rens claimed the world championship, and no one argued. In 1963 the entire team was voted into the Basketball Hall of Fame.

The top players on the Renaissance are also now largely forgotten. But Bob Douglas had an eye for talent when he signed the likes of Clarence "Fat" Jenkins, James "Pappy" Ricks, Charles "Tarzan" Cooper, John "Casey" Holt, Eyre "Bruiser" Saitch, Bill Yancy and Wee Willie Smith. They could play the game and used the same fast-moving style of play as the Celtics.

The Harlem Globetrotters were another black team that began in the late 1920s – 1926 to be exact. The Trotters were the brainchild of Abe Saperstein and were started as strictly another barnstorming team, playing out of the Savoy Ballroom in Chicago. Though Saperstein and his original players were mainly from the Chicago area, their name implied New York. But Saperstein said the "Harlem" was to tell people the team was black and "Globetrotters" to give the impression that the team had been around.

Of course, anyone who follows the game of basketball knows that the Harlem Globetrotters were to become perhaps the most famous team in the world, ambassadors of good will who eventually developed a basketball comedy routine that thrilled and entertained audiences worldwide. They did, indeed, become full-fledged globetrotters, as well as international stars of the first magnitude.

The comedy routines evolved slowly. Signing the best black players available, Saperstein built a team that rarely lost, and fans became bored watching the Trotters beat up on the opposition. To rekindle fan interest, the Trotters began to clown around, developing routines that took remarkable ball-handling and dribbling skills, showcasing the individual talents of such stars as Reece "Goose" Tatum, Marques Haynes and, later, Meadowlark Lemon.

Though the Trotters continued to play competitive basketball right into the 1940s, often opposing teams of college all-stars and even beating the world champion Minneapolis Lakers with George Mikan on occasion, it was their comedy that brought in the box office, and starting in the 1950s the team began concentrating solely on entertainment. By then they were a million dollar business, eventually splitting into two teams, one touring the United States, the other the rest of the world.

But before the Rens and the Trotters began to hit their stride in the 1930s, the Celtics remained the only real stable

OPPOSITE: *The Globetrotters winning a big pro tourney in 1940 over the Bruins of Chicago.*

LEFT: *George Preston Marshall.*

ABOVE: *The rugged Chicago Bruins played in the old American League. On 18 Feb 1927 the Bruins lost a 31-29 game to the Celtics at the Broadway Armory in Chicago.*

professional team playing the game. In 1926 a more-than-usually serious attempt was made to form a professional league that might put basketball on a par with the other professional sports of the time. The driving force behind the new league was George Preston Marshall, who would later become the owner of the NFL Washington Redskins. Marshall called the new league the American Basketball league and started play in 1926-27 with eight teams.

The fly in the ointment was the Celtics. They were doing so well as an independent team that they refused to join the new league. In fact, it wasn't long before they began beating up on some of the ABL team in exhibitions. Finally, George Marshall and his new league president, Joe F Carr (who was also the president of the National Football League), forbade any of the league teams to play the Celtics. Since this would cut into the Celtics' chance for good paydays, the team finally relented and joined the league as its New York entry. Other members were from Baltimore, Chicago, Washington, Cleveland, Fort Wayne, Philadelphia and Rochester.

There was another well-known sportsman connected with the new league: George Halas, the owner of the Chicago Bears football team. Halas also operated the pro

basketball Chicago Bruins, eventually hiring Honey Russell as player-coach. Max Rosenblum, who owned a large department store in Cleveland, was the backer of the franchise from that city, while in Fort Wayne the chamber of commerce ran the team.

When the Celtics joined the ABL in mid-season the Cleveland team was on top, having just edged Washington. But from then on the Celtics began to show their class, winning 19 of their 20 games, then rolling over the Rosenblums in three straight playoff games. They had become the league's first champions.

But there was still animosity. George Marshall had spent some $65,000 trying to buy ballplayers who could beat the Celtics. One night, as the Celtics were routing Marshall's Washington Palace Five, Dutch Dehnert was heard to shout, "We'll break you yet, George."

Washington dropped out after the first year, and in the second season the Celtics finished with a 40-9 record, winning both halves of the season. Then they easily beat Fort Wayne in the playoffs, becoming champions for a second time. The Celtics might have been breaking Marshall, but in a sense, they were also breaking the league. Fans were becoming bored watching the Celtics win so often and so easily. So before the 1929-30 season, the league's third, the ABL anounced that it was "reorganizing."

What that meant, in reality, was that the ABL had decided to break up the Celtics. With the threat of no more pro basketball, the Celtics went along, though owner Jim Donovan was supposedly not even compensated for the dissolution of his powerful franchise. Nat Holman and Davey Banks went to a new New York team known as the Hakoahs and made up totally of Jewish players. Pete Barry and Dutch Dehnert

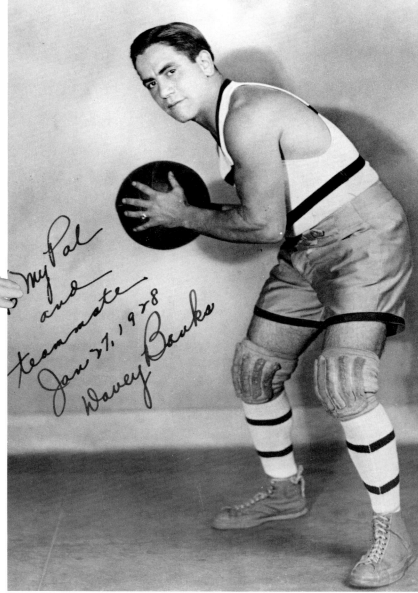

OPPOSITE: *In 1929, the Celtics were split up to try to keep the American League alive. Many of the players went to the Cleveland Rosenblums. Left to right, Davey Banks, Pete Barry, Nat Hickey, Dutch Dehnert, Joe Lapchick and Ed Gillium.*

LEFT: *Joe Lapchick became a key member of the Original Celtics and later a great coach.*

ABOVE: *Little Davey Banks made his reputation playing for Eddie Gottlieb and the Philadelphia SPHAs. Later, he joined the Celtics, though some say the Celtics stole him after Banks had played brilliantly in a best-of-three series won by the SPHAs over the Celtics.*

went to Rochester. Johnny Beckman moved to Baltimore, and Joe Lapchick went to the Cleveland Rosenblums, where he was later joined by Barry and Dehnert. Since the Rosenblums already had two former Celtics, Nat Hickey and Carl Husta, that made them almost a reincarnation of the Celtics. Sure enough, they ran away with the league. There was still no parity, no real intense battle that might have brought in more fans. In addition, president Carr had instituted a "rookie rule," which required that three of the eight players on each team have less than a year's experience in the league, and that two of these rookies always be in the game at all times. The rule made absolutely no sense and only helped dilute the quality of play.

In addition to the rookie rule, which began in 1931, perhaps as an effort to stop the dominance of the Rosenblums, the league also outlawed the pivot play, which Dutch Dehnert played to perfection. Disgusted by the changes, the Rosenblums dropped out of the league by midseason, and by the end of the year the American Basketball League was no more. The fact that the country was entering the Great Depression didn't help either. But no matter what the reasons, professional basketball was still unable to stabilize, unable to organize into one solid, professional league.

Thus about the only thing that was keeping pro basketball alive in the 1920s was the Celtics. Whether called the New York Celtics or Original Celtics, they were pro basketball's first truly dominant team and the first that had widespread recognition. In fact, after the ABL folded a number of the old Celtics players reorganized and began barnstorming once again, traveling in a large second-hand automobile and playing for a guarantee against a percentage of the gate. The pro game still had a long way to go.

ON TO THE NBA

During the 1930s and the early 1940s professional basketball continued to struggle. The sport just couldn't seem to catch on with the general public on a permanent basis. Perhaps, as Eddie Gottlieb once observed, it was because many of the professional teams were actually just club teams. "It wasn't a matter of, say, Philadelphia against New York then," Gottlieb said. "It was the Philadelphia SPHA's against the New York Jewels. There were no rivalries between cities. So the populace at large just didn't get excited about the game."

Yet leagues continued to arise and try to make it work. Two years after folding up in 1931, the American Basketball League revived with a different set of teams, the club teams that Gottlieb had spoken about. The SPHA's were the most dominant team in the league, taking seven titles in 13 years, and the other team that he mentioned, the New York Jewels, was composed of most of the same players who had played for St John's and were nicknamed the "Wonder Five." Club teams for sure, yet somehow the league did manage to stay in business.

Still, it was more or less a weekend league, with the players often paid on a per game basis, just like in the old days. It was still a physical, rough game, and not always for the average college player. Sonny Hertzberg, who played for both the New York Jewels and New York Gothams in the old ABL, recalled that "in pro ball there was always a fist in your chest or a hand in your face. The pros just didn't want a young kid coming in and taking the place of a seasoned old timer."

During this time the players were beginning to get bigger. Centers were averaging about six-feet, six or six-feet, seven, while the forwards were around six, three, though some guards were still little guys. But the game was not as specialized as it is today. Everyone on the court had to do a little of everything. And everyone played defense. Smaller men had to be able to guard and box out

LEFT: *A rough-and-tumble semi-finals match between the Harlem Globetrotters and the Detroit Eagles in 1930. Finally the Eagles won it 37-36.*

OPPOSITE: *Action is hot in this American Basketball League game between the Brooklyn Jewels and the Kate Smith Celtics in 1937. The ABL was essentially a weekend league, with the players part-time pros. But don't tell that to Brooklyn's Sy Spindell as he goes hard to the hoop.*

larger, heavier players. Everyone had to be able to pass, set up plays and, of course, shoot.

Yet while the college game was already attracting large sellout crowds at arenas like Madison Square Garden, the pro game in the second ABL of the 1930s woud pull perhaps 3-7000 fans, depending on the arena and the team. And because it was a weekend league, many of the pro players weren't always in the best of shape.

By 1937 a second professional league had been formed. It was called the National Basketball League and had most of its franchises in small midwestern cities. Some of the small-town teams were Tri-Cities, Oskosh, Waterloo, Flint and Anderson, while other franchises were in larger cities such

as Detroit, Chicago, Minneapolis and Syracuse. This mix of large and small might have kept the NBL from being perceived as a real major league, yet some of the smaller cities hung on to their franchises for years, even when the sport was finally going big time.

Al Cervi, who came from the Buffalo area of New York, was in some way typical of the basketball player of the mid-1930s. Cervi wasn't college bound, but he was an outstanding athlete who had to give up baseball after suffering an arm injury. He would eventually play in the early days of the NBA with the Rochester Royals, but his road there was sometimes paved with frustration, as well as with a variety of diversified basketball experiences. "I played all the rules, the old ones and the new," Cervi said. "The net game was interesting, with the ball in play all the time, and must have been a good game. But I really didn't like the old double dribble."

By 1938 Cervi was a member of the Buffalo Bisons and playing in the National Basketball League. Yet after he played an exhibition game against a team from Rochester, Les Harrison of Rochester asked Cervi to also play for his club, called the Rochestern Pros at the time. He could still double up, because the Rochester team was in the New York State League. So nothing much had changed. Pro basketball was still a loose grouping of many leagues, with players still acting as gypsy athletes, finding a game, even a new league, wherever they could.

But then World War II came along, and when it ended much had changed. Tired of the long war and the stories of death and destruction, people looked to sports as one of the many ways to forget. With pro stars returning from the service, baseball and football fans were more than ready to go out and root for their old favorites — they hadn't seen some players perform for nearly four seasons — and professional sports were in for a new post-war boom.

And that once again raised the question of basketball. Here it was 1945, and there still wasn't a bona fide big league for the sport, which was now more than half a century old. The American League was still operating weekends on the East Coast, while the Midwest had the National League, yet some teams were still sponsored by

LEFT: *With still no strong pro league in the 1930s, semi-pro games existed everywhere. Here is action from a game between the Washington, D C, "Y" and the New York West Side "Y" in March 1936. Washington won the game 45-26. Note the brick wall to the side of the court.*

OPPOSITE: *New York Whirlwinds (dark jerseys) battle a team called the Brewers in ABL action in 1936. The player grabbing the rebound is also being fouled. Even though pro players didn't make much money then, they still had to be tough. In fact, they played a much rougher game than did their college counterparts.*

companies or industries and didn't represent even an entire city or area.

Then, early in 1946, things began changing. According to Eddie Gottlieb and others, the idea for a new kind of big league began with Max Kase, the sports editor of the New York *Journal American* and the same man who would be instrumental in exposing college basketball's first major scandal a few years later. "Max Kase went around to a lot of different people to see if there was interest in another pro basketball league," Eddie Gottlieb recalled some 30 years later. "At first he didn't have much luck, but then he got the idea of talking to the major arena owners, trying to convince them that pro basketball would give them another event to put into their buildings two nights a week, keeping the buildings open and the concessions busy at the same time."

One of the first men to go along with the idea was Walter Brown, who was the president of the Boston Garden and owner of the Boston Bruins of the National Hockey League. Once Brown said yes, other arena owners followed. Yet one prominent owner balked at first. Ned Irish of Madison Square Garden said he would not become part of a new professional league. "It was Arthur Wirtz in Chicago who convinced Irish to come into the league," Gottlieb recalled. "He simply told him if he didn't join and someone else got the New York franchise, Irish would be left out in the cold, especially if the league was a success."

So Irish came into the fold. It was an important step, because many felt that if the new league didn't include the Garden it was doomed to failure. On 6 June 1946 the arena owners met in New York and officially formed the Basketball Association of America. To solidify the new league even further the owners chose Maurice Podoloff as its first president. Podoloff was a Connecticut lawyer who was serving as president of the American Hockey League at the time,

and he clearly had the experience.

That fall the BAA began play with 11 teams located in New York, Boston, Philadelphia, Washington, Chicago, St Louis, Cleveland, Pittsburgh, Detroit, Providence and Toronto. Some of the names are familiar: New York Knickerbockers, Boston Celtics, Philadelphia Warriors. But though the ABL died with the formation of the BAA, the NBL continued to play in the small midwestern cities where it had operated since 1937. The National League was not about to call it quits just because a new league had formed. They would continue play and bid for players.

The new league went about its business. It didn't like the college game of two 20-minute halves. Instead, it set up four 12-minute quarters, a standard still used today. And in the first season it outlawed the zone defense, looking to provide a more wide-open, entertaining game. The man-to-man is still the only legal defense in the National Basketball Association today.

The BAA picked up players quickly. There were those returning from the war looking for a way to play the game once again. Others came from the old American League. And ballplayers coming out of college also figured that they might have a place to play pro ball if the league succeeded, so why not give it a try. There was really no early battle for players between the BAA and NBL. The two leagues were smart enough not to get into a bidding war, and they only doubled up in a couple of cities, Detroit and Chicago. Otherwise, the NBL franchises were in Rochester, Fort Wayne, Syracuse, Toledo, Indianapolis, Oshkosh, Sheboygan, Anderson, Moline and Youngstown.

It was soon obvious that both the BAA and NBL were pro leagues playing a fine brand of basketball. And each had its share of star players. Jumpin' Joe Fulks of the Philadelphia Warriors was the BAA's first scoring champion. The ex-Marine averaged 23.2 points a game, with a high of 41

OPPOSITE: *By 1946 the Basketball Association of America had begun play. This league would eventualy become the NBA. There were 11 teams the first year, most playing in large arenas. In the action here, Mickey Rottner of the Chicago Stags drives to the hoop as the New York Knicks' Sonny Hertzberg (8) and Leo Gottlieb (9) look to top him.*

ABOVE: *The Philadelphia Warriors were the first BAA champs of 1946-7. Seated, l to r, Jerry Rullo, Angelo Musi, Pete Tyrell, Pete Rosenberg, Jerry Fleishman. Standing, l to r, Cy Kaselman, George Senesky, Ralph Kaplowitz, Howard Dallmar, Art Hillhouse, Joe Fulks, Matt Guokas, and Coach Eddie Gottlieb.*

RIGHT: *Sportswriter Max Kase, who helped uncover college basketball's first scandal, also played a big role in starting the BAA.*

points against Toronto. He finished the season with a scoring lead of more than 400 points over runner-up Bob Feerick of Washington.

Feerick was also a BAA All-Star, as was his Washington teammate, Bones McKinney. And their team, the Capitols, was coached by Arnold "Red" Auerbach, who would later become perhaps the most well known pro basketball coach of all-time, a reputation made after he moved over to the Boston Celtics.

But Auerbach could coach even then, as his Washington team finished the regular season with a 49-11 record, some 14 games ahead of Philadelphia in the East. Chicago won the West by one game over St Louis, compiling a 39-22 log. Max Zaslofsky, with a 14.4 scoring average, was also an All-Star and the leader of the Chicago team.

In the playoffs, however, Eddie Gottlieb's Warriors emerged as the first league champion after the Chicago Stags upset the Capitols in the semi-finals. The Warriors topped the St Louis Bombers, then the New York Knickerbockers, before beating Chicago four games to one for the title.

A few quick notes about that first BAA season. While Fulks led all scorers with a 23.2 average, he did it by hitting 475 of 1557 shots, which translates to a shooting percentage of only 30.5 percent. Today's top pros usually shoot at a 50 percent or better clip, with some hitting more than 60 percent of their field goal tries. In addition, the assists leader was Ernie Calverly of the Providence Steamrollers, with 3.4 assists per game. Today the top playmakers average more than 10 assists a game. It's certainly an interesting comparison, showing how the game has changed and how the individual skill level has improved.

At the same time, the National Basketball League was making some noise of its own. Determined not to be considered a minor league because the BAA was in the larger cities with the larger arenas, the NBL went out and signed George Mikan, the six-foot, ten-inch center out of De Paul. Mikan had actually turned down an offer from the NBL Chicago Gears a year earlier, but in 1946-47 he decided to turn pro, signing a five-year deal worth some $60,000, a huge amount for a basketball player at that time.

It didn't take Mikan long before he became a dominant player. He averaged 16.5 points a game his first year and became the league's Most Valuable Player. The Gears finished third in the regular season, but with Mikan leading the way, they went on to win the playoffs. But the league had a rule of awarding the championship to the team with the best record, so the Rochester Royals, with All-Stars Al Cervi and Bob Davies, were declared league champions. Joining Mikan, Cervi and Davies on the league All-Star team were Bobby McDermott of Chicago and Fred Lewis of Sheboygan.

A year later the uncertainties inherent in a new basketball league were plainly in evidence, as the BAA lost four teams, Toronto, Cleveland, Pittsburgh and Detroit. Though the BAA added one new club, Baltimore, to become an eight-team circuit, some people already felt it was just a matter of time before the new league folded.

OPPOSITE: *Bob Davies (11) of the Rochester Royals goes in for two against the Knicks.*

LEFT: *George Mikan of the Lakers throws up a hook over "Sweetwater" Clifton of the Knicks.*

ABOVE: *The BAA's first scoring champion, Joe Fulks of Philadelphia, goes hard to the basket in an early BAA game against St Louis. Fulks averaged 23.2 points a game in 1946-7, the only player to average more than 20 and score more than 1000 points.*

155

But it hung on, cutting the schedule back from 60 games to just 48. And the money wasn't great, either. The average salary those first years was about $4500 a man, with the championship offering a bonus of an additional $2000 a man. Cutting the schedule back to 48 games didn't help, for it cost the arena owners 12 dates, and for a league struggling to survive, the loss of a dozen games could be costly.

Yet the BAA made it through a second season. A New York Knicks rookie named Carl Braun set a new record by scoring 47 points against Providence, and Joe Fulks once again had the highest scoring average, with a 22.1 mark. Max Zaslofsky had a 21.0 average, but scored the most points, with 1007. The big surprise was in the playoffs, when the new Baltimore team won the championship by upsetting Philadelphia in the finals four games to two.

Yet it was in the NBL during the 1947-48 season where events were taking place that would most effect the future of professional basketball. For starters, Morris White, owner of the Chicago Gears, had a dispute with the league and withdrew his franchise. At the same time, the Detroit franchise, which had won just four of 44 games the season before, moved to Minneapolis, where it took the new nickname of the Lakers. And in a draft of the Chicago players, the Lakers received George Mikan, as well as another All-Star-caliber player, Jim Pollard.

The addition of Mikan and Pollard, as well as several other new players, transformed the new Minneapolis franchise into an immediate winner. With Mikan becoming even more dominant in his second season, the Lakers won the NBL championship, as Mikan took the scoring title with a 21.3 average and won the league MVP prize. Pollard was also an all-star, as well as rookie Marko Todorovich of

LEFT: *When George Mikan (99) joined the Lakers, he began to dominate the pro game just as he had dominated college ball earlier. In this 1949 playoff game against the Washington Capitols, Mikan scores over Dick O'Keefe (13) of the Caps, as teammates Arnie Ferrin (18) and Jim Pollard (17) look on.*

OPPOSITE: *In 1949 the BAA and NBL merged to become the National Basketball Association. In the center of the photo, Maurice Podoloff, first NBA Commissioner. On the left, Eddie Gottlieb, the great basketball pioneer, who was then the coach of the Philadelphia Warriors and a member of the old BAA Executive Board.*

Sheboygan and a pair of Rochester stars, Al Cervi and Red Holzman, who would also gain fame later as a coach.

But before the next season could begin, the face of professional basketball would change once again. During the offseason BAA president Podoloff decided to make a bold move. Using as bait the fact that his league operated in the big cities and arenas, he began trying to induce NBL teams to switch leagues. First Indianapolis and Fort Wayne switched allegiance. They were followed by the NBL's new flagship franchise, Minneapolis, and finally by Rochester. The defections sounded the death knell of the NBL, though they would survive for one more season.

The new teams swelled the BAA ranks to 12 teams, and the league began its 1948-49 season with renewed optimism. All four former NBL teams were placed in the Western Division, and when the smoke cleared, Rochester and Minneapolis had the best records in the entire league, Mikan had beaten out Fulks for the scoring title with a 28.3 average and Bob Davies led the league in assists, averaging 5.4 a game. When the playoffs ended, it was the Minneapolis Lakers who were BAA champions, defeating the Washington Capitols in six games.

It had been an exciting season. The success of both the Rochester and Minneapolis teams had shown everyone that the NBL had been a quality league, and the additions had only served to make the BAA that much stronger. Other top pro players during that important season were Arnie Risen of Rochester, Ed Sadowski of Philadelphia, Ken Sailors of Providence, Carl Braun of New York, Andy Phillip of Chicago, Bob Wanzer of Rochester and George Senesky of Philadelphia. Add Mikan, Pollard, Davies, Fulks, Feerick, McKinney, Zaslofsky and Ernie Calverly to the list, and basketball fans realized that there was a whole group of outstanding pro players upon which to build a new league.

During the offseason the NBL officially died, and the remaining viable teams merged into the BAA for 1949-50. The league found itself with 17 teams crammed into three divisions. That seemed to be too many, especially since some were small-city teams such as Tri-Cities, Sheboygan, Waterloo and Anderson. Something would eventually have to be done, but for the moment, 17 it would be.

And there was something else that was changed before 1949-50. From now on, the BAA would have a new name. It would be called the National Basketball Association.

THE FIRST DYNASTY

A 17-team league: In some ways, it was a joke. After all, professional basketball was still struggling for stability. Suddenly two leagues merge and there are 17 pro teams, more than in major league baseball, which had already been on the books for nearly half a century. One explanation was that the new NBA had to take all the NBL teams to avoid legal action. They could then slowly weed them out or just let them fold up and hope the core of the league would survive.

The Eastern Division was still solid, with Syracuse of the NBL joining New York, Washington, Philadelphia, Baltimore and Boston. The Central Divison had Minneapolis, Rochester, Fort Wayne, Chicago and St Louis, the first three all being former NBL teams. But the Western Division was something of a fifth wheel, with Anderson, Tri-Cities, Sheboygan, Waterloo and Denver. However, there was also a new team in the West. The Indianapolis Olympians joined the league in 1949-50, and they were led by former Kentucky stars Alex Groza and Ralph Beard. The Olympians would surprise everyone by winning their division.

Mikan, of course, was the NBA's first real superstar and dominant big man. In fact, some people still feel that Mikan was the one player who really saved the league in the early years. He would lead the NBA in scoring, with a 27.4 average. Rookie Groza was the only other player to average more than 20 points a game that year, scoring at a 23.4 clip. Yet the league's best record belonged to another NBL team, the Syracuse Nationals. The Nats won the East with a 51-13 mark and were a club that featured high-scoring Dolph Schayes and veteran Al Cervi. Minneapolis and Rochester tied for the Central Division crown with idetical marks of 51-17. And those three teams – Syracuse, Minneapolis and Rochester – started a trend that still characterizes great NBA teams today: They were extremely difficult to defeat on their home courts, each club losing only a single home game all year.

The Lakers broke the Central Division tie with a 78-76 victory over the Royals, then went on to win the champion-

ship, defeating Syracuse in the finals in six tough games. Led by Mikan, Jim Pollard, Vern Mikkelsen, Arnie Ferrin and little Slater Martin, the Lakers were a talented crew who would be hard to beat. Mikan and Pollard were joined on the All-Star team by Max Zaslofsky of Chicago, Bobby Davies of Rochester, and rookie Alex Groza of Indianapolis.

During the offseason the league made some strides toward stabilization. Chicago, Anderson, Denver, St Louis, Waterloo and Sheboygan all folded their franchises, while Washington disbanded early in the following year after losing Coach Red Auerbach to the Boston Celtics. It was also the year in which the first black players – Chuck Cooper of Boston, Nat "Sweetwater" Clifton of New York and Earl Lloyd of Washington – came into the league.

There was still another interesting rookie joining the NBA in 1950-51. His name was Bob Cousy, an all-American guard from Holy Cross. Cousy was six feet, one inch, but with players already getting bigger, some thought he might be too small for rugged NBA play. Yet Cousy had extremely sturdy legs, long arms and very strong wrists. Those assets enabled him to become a master dribbler and ball-handler, one of the first players to use the behind-the-back dribble with regularity and without breaking stride.

Cousy was originally drafted by the old Tri-Cities franchise out in Illinois. His first reaction was "What's a Tri-City?" and he thought seriously about passing up pro ball and going into business. But he finally signed, only to find himself traded to Chicago before the season began. Then the Chicago franchise folded, and Cousy's name was put in

OPPOSITE: *The ill-fated Indianapolis Olympians. The franchise debuted in 1949 and featured stars of the great Kentucky Wildcat teams of the 1940s. Left to right, Wah Wah Jones, Cliff Barker, Alex Groza and Ralph Beard. Groza and Beard were later banned from the NBA for their role in the college scandals. Shortly after that, the franchise folded.*

TOP RIGHT: *The great Dolph Schayes of the Syracuse Nats, one of the best players and top foul shooters in NBA history. A 6-8 forward, he could go underneath or shoot a long, two-hand set from the outside.*

RIGHT: *George Mikan was never too big to go after a loose ball. Here the big guy out-hustles the Knicks' Irv Rothenberg (3) and Mel Magaha in December 1948.*

159

a hat along with those of two other players. That's when he was chosen by the Boston Celtics, the team he originally wanted, and he eagerly joined the Celts and their new coach, Red Auerbach.

There were a number of additional significant events during the 1950-51 season. On 22 November the Fort Wayne Pistons traveled to Minneapolis to play the Lakers. Under ordinary circumstances the Pistons just didn't have the firepower to stay with George Mikan and company, so they tried something different, a slowdown game to end all slowdown games. The Pistons stalled and stalled and then stalled some more. While the 7000 fans booed continuously, the Pistons proceeded to win the lowest-scoring game in NBA history, beating the Lakers by a 19-18 count.

The league didn't want this kind of strategy to become the norm, especially against Mikan, who had become the NBA's number one gate attraction. It took several more years before the league insured that this kind of thing wouldn't happen again. But when the league finally installed the 24-second clock in 1954-55, making it necessary for a team to get a shot off within 24 seconds, most observers felt the rule was a direct result of the 19-18 game of 1950.

Though the Lakers had the league's best record at the end of the season, they were upset in the semi-finals of the playoffs by the Rochester Royals, who took the best of five series in four games. Then Royals then went on to defeat the New York Knicks in seven games to become the new NBA champions. Mikan was again the runaway scoring leader, hitting at a 28.4 clip. Alex Groza of Indianapolis and Easy Ed Macauley of Boston were the only other players to average more than 20 points a game. As for rookie Cousy, he had broken in with a bang, averaging 15.6 points a game and finishing fourth in the league in assists, with 4.9 a game. He had quickly proven himself a top player, as well as a top gate attraction.

At the end of the 1950-51 season the NBA presented its first All-Star Game. More than 10,000 fans flocked to the Boston Garden to see the East stars play against the West. The East won 111-94, with Macauley scoring 20 points, Joe Fulks 19 and Paul Arizin and Dolph Schayes 15 each. For the West, Groza popped for 17 points and 13 rebounds, while Mikan was held to just 12. Tricky Dick McGuire of New York and Cousy were the winning team's best playmakers, with ten and eight assists. The league had taken

LEFT: *Slater Martin was a 5-10 playmaker who really made the championship Lakers go. While at the University of Texas, Martin once scored 49 points in a single game. So he could put the ball in the hoop when he had to. But more often with the Lakers he was setting up the likes of Mikan, Jim Pollard and Vern Mikkelsen.*

OPPOSITE: *Slender "Easy" Ed Macauley was a 6-8 forward who starred in the NBA for St Louis and Boston from 1949 to 1959. He averaged more than 17 points a game for his career, but he will probably be more remembered for a trade. In 1956 he went from Boston to St Louis in a deal that enabled the Celtics to get the rights to the great Bill Russell.*

still another step toward respectability.

For the next three years there was very little franchise movement, with the exception of Tri-Cities moving to Milwaukee in 1951. And in those three years the Minneapolis Lakers dominated professional basketball. Led by the 250-pound Mikan, the Lakers won three consecutive NBA championships, defeating New York twice and then Syracuse in the final rounds. Coach John Kundla built his great team around the nucleus of Mikan, six-foot, seven-inch Mikkelsen, six-foot, three-inch Pollard and five-foot, ten-inch Slater Martin. But he also had other fine ballplayers in Whitey Skoog, Dick Schnittker and Clyde Lovellette.

Yet despite the Lakers' dominance, there was a host of fine new ballplayers entering the NBA during the days of the Minneapolis dynasty. Philadelphia forward Paul Arizin displaced Mikan as the league's scoring king in 1951-52, averaging 25.4 points per game, while Cousy had his average up to 21.2. A year later Philly center Neil Johnston was the top point-getter, with Mikan second once again. The league did lose a pair of top players after 1951 when Commissioner Podoloff suspended Indianapolis' Alex Groza and Ralph Beard for their part in the college basketball scandals while at Kentucky. They would never play again, and by 1953-54 the Indianapolis franchise was gone as well.

But a glance at the rosters at the end of 1954 show a brace

ABOVE: *Another title for the Lakers. A happy group of Minneapolis Lakers celebrate the 1953 NBA title after they bested the New York Knicks in seven games. In the photo are George Mikan (99) and Slater Martin (22).*

RIGHT: *Philadelphia's Paul Arizin was one of the great NBA scorers of the 1950s. Arizin averaged more than 22 points a game for his career.*

OPPOSITE: *Vern Mikkelsen, right, was a regular on the powerful Minneapolis Lakers team that George Mikan led into the decade of the 1950s. As such, he was to become a member of the game's first dynasty.*

of outstanding ballplayers now playing professional basketball and beginning to help the NBA slowly earn the respect of its critics. Besides the aforementioned players, other new NBA stars included Bill Sharman of Boston, Larry Foust and Mel Hutchins of Fort Wayne, Harry Gallatin of New York, Arnie Risen of Rochester, Paul Seymour of Syracuse and Jack George of Philadelphia.

Shortly after the 1953-54 season ended, a surprise announcement came out of Minneapolis: George Mikan was retiring from basketball shortly before his 30th birthday. Though the Lakers were a solid team right down to the end of the bench, they wouldn't be the same without the big guy. Mikan did make a brief comeback two years later to try to help the Lakers at the gate, but he was no longer the same decisive force. He had led the Minneapolis Lakers to five titles in six years, spanning three different leagues — the NBL, BAA and NBA. There was no question that he was the dominant player of his generation. With Mikan gone, however, the race to the NBA title was wide open, and the 1954-55 season was looked upon with great expectations.

There was a major rule change before the 1954-55 season began, and that was the 24-second rule. The league also tried to cut back on excessive fouling by limiting teams to six fouls a quarter. Anything after that and there would be a bonus free throw awarded.

In addition, two outstanding rookies had come into the league, and they both wound up on the same team, the Milwaukee Hawks. One was a rugged six-foot, nine-inch forward from Louisiana State, Bob Pettit, and the other a six-foot, three-inch guard from Furman, Frank Selvy. Both had been outstanding players in college. In fact, Selvy had set that amazing record by scoring 100 points in a game. Selvy actually started with Baltimore, but when the franchise folded he came to join Pettit at Milwaukee. The league

OPPOSITE TOP: *Dolph Schayes of Syracuse drives in for a layup between a pair of New York Knicks in a 1954 game. Caught out by Schayes' quick move are Harry Gallatin (11) and Sweetwater Clifton (8).*

OPPOSITE BOTTOM: *George Mikan posing for a publicity shot in 1948. At 6-10, big George could dunk with ease, yet he would almost seem small if matched against some of the giants of today.*

RIGHT: *Milwaukee rookies Bob Pettit (8) and Frank Selvy (13) were terrific their first year in the NBA. Here, they perform in the 1955 All-Star Game at Madison Square Garden.*

BOTTOM RIGHT: *Electrifying Bob Cousy was perhaps the most exciting player of his time, the quarterback who directed the early years of the Celtics dynasty. Here the Cooz goes airborne.*

was down to eight teams, but the quality of play was getting better, and over the next five years the number of impact players entering the league would astound people.

The team that would eventually replace Minneapolis as the league champion in 1954-55 was the Syracuse Nationals. Led by six-foot, eight-inch forward Dolph Schayes, the Nats had some fine ballplayers. They were coached by the dynamic Al Cervi, who had been an all-pro in the old NBL. He got the most out of players such as center John Kerr, forwards Red Rocha and Earl Lloyd and guards Paul Seymour and George King.

In the playoff finals that year the Nats went up against the Fort Wayne Pistons, another fine team. Led by six-foot, nine-inch center Larry Foust, the Pistons had some other talented players, forwards George Yardley and Mel Hutchins, for example, and guards Max Zaslofsky and Andy Phillip. It was a series in which the home team won each game. And in the seventh and final contest the Syracuse team won by a single point, 92-91, to succeed the Lakers as NBA champs.

Though many of the NBA cast remained the same in 1954-55, there were several significant developments. The Milwaukee Hawks' super rookie, Bob Pettit, was brilliant enough to finish fourth in the league in scoring, with a 20.4 average, and his rookie teammate, Frank Selvy, was next, at 19.0. Pettit was also tied for second in rebounds, behind Philadelphia's Neil Johnston. But he represented just the beginning, as more rookies would soon follow, many making an immediate impact upon the game.

In addition, Bob Cousy was on his way to becoming the NBA's most exciting performer. He was third in the league in scoring, behind Philly's Johnston and Arizin, averaging 21.2 points a game. He also led the league in assists, with 7.8 a game, and many of them of the spectacular variety,

his behind-the-back passes and unique ways of making a play thrilling fans throughout the league.

With Easy Ed Macauley and Bill Sharman joining Cousy, the Celtics had a trio of all-league players. Yet despite their three stalwarts and Coach Red Auerbach, the Celts were still just a .500 team. They needed something, a final piece to the puzzle, and though no one knew it at the time, the missing piece was just two years away.

The times they were a-changing. At the outset of the 1955-56 season there was just a single player remaining from the BAA's initial season some ten years earlier. He was Connie Simmons of Rochester. The only other remaining BAA pioneer player, the Pistons' Max Zaslofsky, had been

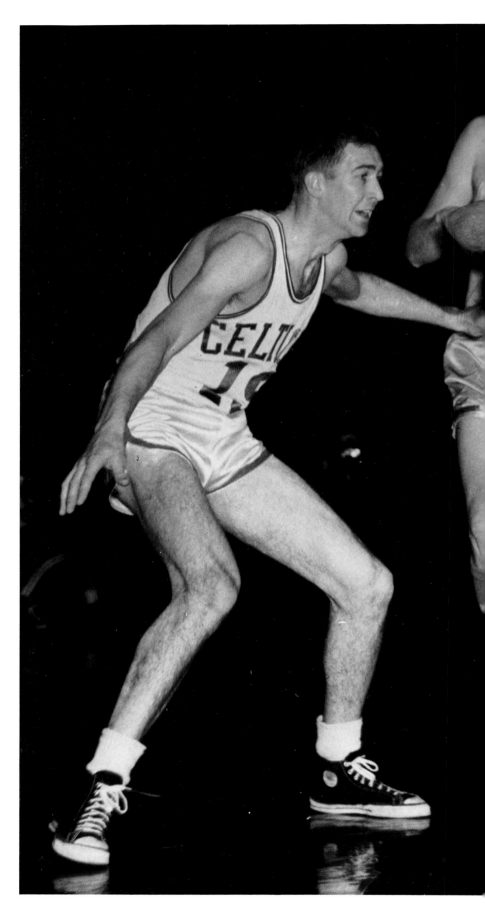

waived before the season started.

It was also the season in which Bob Pettit became a super-star. With the Hawks now playing out of St Louis, Pettit was absolutely brilliant. He won the scoring title, with a 25.7 average, and also led the league in rebounding, gathering caroms at a 16.2 clip. He became the league's first Most Valuable Player and was also the outstanding player in the All-Star Game that year. The Rookie of the Year was six-foot, seven-inch Maurice Stokes, out of tiny St Francis College, who almost beat out Pettit for the rebound crown.

But the league champion was Philadelphia. The Warriors had put together a fine team, led by the high-scoring duo of Neil Johnston and Paul Arizin. Complementing them were forward Joe Graboski and guards Jack George and Tom Gola. Gola was the six-foot, six-inch rookie from La Salle who had been a three-time collegiate all-American. He came

OPPOSITE: *Bob Pettit of the Hawks is still considered one of the best all-round forwards ever to have played the game. The 6-9 Pettit out of LSU could score and rebound, was a leader and fierce competitor. He was also a multiple scoring champion and in 1958 led St Louis to the NBA title. In the sixth and final game against Boston that year, Petit scored 50 points, including 19 of his team's final 21.*

LEFT: *Pro basketball at its best in the middle 1950s. Whitey Skoog (20) of the Lakers dribbles past Bill Sharman (21) of the Celtics as Boston's Arnie Risen (19) prepares to pick him up. In the background is big Clyde Lovellette of the Lakers. The game took place in 1955, as the Laker dynasty was winding down and just before Bill Russell joined the Celtics to begin their run of titles.*

into the NBA just in time to complete the Warrior quintet and help them to a title.

After making the transition from college superstar to professional, Tom Gola noted the differences between the college and pro game of the middle 1950s. Looking back years later he said that while the college players were often quick to avoid contact, the pros were always looking for contact to break a guy loose. Bob Pettit, too, testified as to the physical nature of the pro game. "At the beginning I was six, nine and weighed only 195 pounds, and I took a tremendous physical pounding until I could develop more strength. I began lifting weights and eventually played at about 240 pounds. Before that, some of the veteran players tried to intimidate me . . . . There were a plain lot of rough customers around."

That was the NBA game during the so-called Mikan era.

Perhaps big George was the most symbolic of it because he was the most successful. Not very fast or quick, lacking in finesse, Mikan used his strength to get the job done. And he paid for it in bumps, bruises and some broken bones. But, slowly, the league changed things. There was the 24-second rule to speed things up, no zone defenses, the penalty shot after a sixth team foul. It was all designed to improve the quality of the game and bring it into the modern era.

The league was ten years old and the progress had been relatively slow. There were just eight teams, and it would stay that way for another six years. No one was rushing things. It had taken pro ball too long even to become established. But the Mikan era had at last seen to that. Now the game was about to enter a new era, one that in many ways can be considered a golden age.

THE AGE OF THE CELTICS

The age of the Celtics began with Red Auerbach. The coach of the Boston Celtics desperately wanted his team to be a big winner. Actually, the team had done very well in the 1950s with the high-scoring trio of Bob Cousy, Bill Sharman and Easy Ed Macauley. But while the run and gun Celts were usually a winning team and high up in the standings, they had never won an NBA title. Something was missing, and before the 1956-57 season got underway Red Auerbach thought he had the answer.

The man he wanted was Bill Russell, the six-foot, nine-inch All-American center from the University of San Francisco. The big guy's game was defense and rebounding, and that was the element Auerbach felt his high-flying outfit needed. Russell had led the Dons to a pair of NCAA titles, and Auerbach was certain he could do the same thing for the Celtics. The problem was that the Celts had only the sixth pick in the upcoming draft. What if some other team grabbed Russell before them?

Rochester had the first pick that year, but Auerbach knew the Royals didn't have the kind of money Russell would demand. St Louis had the next choice, and Auerbach wasn't sure whether Hawks owner Ben Kerner would take Russell, but he wasn't about to take any chances. He quickly offered Kerner Easy Ed Macauley, a St Louis University graduate, for the draft pick. But Kerner wanted more and Auerbach had to throw in Cliff Hagan, a talented

six-foot, four-inch forward who was about to come out of military service. That's when the deal was made, allowing the Celtics to pick Bill Russell.

Though Russell was committed to playing for the United States Olympic team in Melbourne that year and wouldn't be available until December, Auerbach was willing to wait. Meantime, he also used the old territorial pick (a team had first choice of a college star from its area) to grab Tom Heinsohn, a hot-shooting six-foot, seven-inch forward from Holy Cross. And he also had another service returnee in Frank Ramsey, who had played with Cliff Hagan at Kentucky. Ramsey was a six-foot, three-inch swing man who would become the first of the Celtics' fabled "sixth men," a player who could come off the bench and ignite a team with his scoring and all-round play.

BELOW: *The first Boston Celtics championship came in 1957. Red Auerbach (center) and his Celtics would win many more.*

OPPOSITE TOP: *Bill Russell, hooking over Larry Foust of the Lakers, was the final link in the Celtic chain.*

OPPOSITE BOTTOM: *Coach Red Auerbach and a youthful Tom Heinsohn celebrate the moment of victory as the Celtics eliminate the St Louis Hawks in the double overtime of the seventh game 125-123.*

Though Russell missed about a third of the season, he made an impact as soon as he joined the ballclub. Doing exactly what Auerbach had envisioned, only maybe even better, the big guy became an immediate force in the middle. In fact, he became *the* force in the middle, without a doubt the NBA's best rebounder and shot-blocker. His presence enabled the rest of the Celts to gamble on defense, to press, to trap, to go for the steal. For if the gamble failed, and a man got free in the middle, Russell was there with his great quickness, his long arms and his impeccable timing, and more often than not he would swat the hoped-for open shot away.

With Russell in the lineup, Heinsohn having a great rookie year at shooting forward, big Jim Loscutoff doing the rugged inside work at big forward and Cousy and Sharman working their magic in the backcourt, the Celtics quickly became the class of the NBA. They wound up with a 44-28 record in the regular season, best in the entire league.

The playoffs saw the Celts eliminate the Syracuse Nats in three straight games. They looked unbeatable. But in the finals, the St Louis Hawks gave Boston all they could handle. The series lasted seven hard-fought games. Besides a superstar in Bob Pettit, the Hawks had the likes of Slater Martin and Jack McMahon at guards, six-foot, 11-inch Charley Share at center and Easy Ed Macauley at the other forward. Cliff Hagan, like Ramsey, was brilliant as the sixth man. In other words, the Hawks were good.

The seventh and final game was played at Boston that year, and it was the kind of finish that must have won legions of new fans for the NBA. Pettit was playing with a cast on his left wrist because of a broken bone, but he had

lost little of his effectiveness. With six seconds left, the former LSU star hit a pair of free throws to tie the game at 103 and send it into overtime.

Both teams were playing near to exhaustion, but neither would quit. With just nine seconds left and the Celts up by two, the Hawks' Jack Coleman hit a jumper to tie it once again at 113 and send it into a second overtime. The fans at ancient Boston Garden were hoarse from screaming but got ready to scream some more. And once more the two teams went at it. With just two seconds left, the Celtics again had a slim lead, 125-123. But the Hawks had a ball and one more chance.

Their playing coach, Alex Hannum, decided to gamble by throwing the inbounds pass at the backboard and hope Pettit could outmuscle Russell for the rebound. Sure enough, Pettit got the ball, but when he tried to toss it in the basket before the buzzer the ball fell short. The Celtics had won the game and were world champions.

OPPOSITE: *Cliff Hagan of the St Louis Hawks played a lot taller than his 6-4 height. Hagan could hook with either hand and often played inside with the big guys. Along with Bob Pettit and Clyde Lovellette, Hagan helped keep the Hawks among the NBA's best teams for many years.*

RIGHT: *Alex Hannum was a solid pro forward, beginning his career with Oshkosh of the old NBL. He became a coach, leading the St Louis Hawks to the NBA title in '58.*

BELOW: *Bob Cousy receives the MVP trophy for his play in the 1954 All-Star Game.*

The postseason awards were an indication of what was to come. Bob Cousy was named the league's Most Valuable Player, while Tommy Heinsohn won the Rookie of the Year prize. (That undoubtedly would have gone to Russell, had he not missed the first third of the season for the Olympics.) And while Maurice Stokes of Rochester won the rebounding title with 1256, for a 17.4 average, Russell's 943 were good for fourth place, though his average of 19.3 caroms per game was the best in the NBA. Bill Sharman had averaged 21.1 points a game, Cousy 20.6, Heinsohn 16.2. They were a team to be reckoned with.

A year later, the Celtics again had the best record in the league, as Auerbach continued to build his team, adding 6-4 guard Sam Jones, who would soon become a star in his own right. Russell showed no letup, averaging 22.7 rebounds a game en route to a Most Valuable Player performance. It seemed almost a foregone conclusion that the Celts would take another title. That is, until Russell sprained an ankle in the third game of the final against St Louis.

The club hung on, winning the fourth game without the big guy, but after that they really began feeling his loss. St Louis had a 3-2 lead, and in the sixth game, after Russell tested the ankle and couldn't go, the Celtics were once again without him. Yet they battled the Hawks close all the way, and had it not been for the absolute brilliance of Bob Pettit, they might have pulled it out. But the six-foot, nine-inch sharpshooter was hot and wanted the ball. He scored 19 of his team's final 21 points en route to a record-breaking 50-point performance that not only gave his team a 110-109

victory but gave them the world's championship as well.

It was probably just as well that the Hawks could savor their victory, because it would be the last time any team other than the Boston Celtics would win the NBA championship for the next eight years. The Celtic dynasty was about to roll into high gear.

There was one very tragic development in 1958. The Royals' outstanding young forward, Maurice Stokes, in the midst of his finest season, was stricken with encephalitis, a crippling brain disease that would not only end his career but lead to his premature death some years later.

Cousy, Sharman and Pettit were joined on the All-Star team by Adolph Schayes and George Yardley. Strangely enough, league MVP Russell was placed on the second team by the votes of the sportwriters. Figure that one out. Anyone who knew basketball could tell you that the big center had revolutionized the game, and his defense, rebounding and shotblocking were the prime reasons the Celtics were becoming basketball's best team.

While there were still just eight teams in the NBA, the league was slowly ridding itself of the old smalltown image. Prior to 1957-58 the Rochester franchise was moved to Cincinnati, and the Fort Wayne team had gone over to Detroit. Also during that year, George Yardley of the new Detroit Pistons had become the first player in league history to score more than 2000 points in a season, finishing with 2001 and a 27.4 average.

In the ensuing years there would be many exciting individual stories coming out of the National Basketball Association, but the story team would continue to be the Boston Celtics. The league got a preview in 1958-59 when the Celts finished the regular season at 52-20, three games better than Western Division St Louis. And while Bob Pettit set a new scoring mark, with 2105 points and a 29.2 average, beating out Jack Twyman of Cincinnati, Paul Arizin of Philadelphia and a sensational rookie forward of the Minneapolis Lakers who came to them out of Seattle University, Elgin Baylor, Russell still led the league in rebounding by a wide margin, and Cousy was still the top assist man.

When Minneapolis upset St Louis in the semi-finals, the stage was set. The Celtics swept the Lakers in four straight to regain the NBA crown, the first time a league final was decided by a sweep.

Then, a year later, a new major force arrived on the scene. He was Wilt Chamberlain, the seven-foot, one-inch,

275-pound center from Kansas who had spent a year with the Harlem Globetrotters waiting to become eligible for the NBA. Chamberlain became a territorial pick of the Philadelphia Warriors, and many felt the big guy's presence would enable the Warriors to challenge Russell and the Celts for NBA supremacy.

Chamberlain did take the NBA by storm. The most imposing physical player of his time, and maybe all time, the Big Dipper set new scoring and rebounding records in his rookie season. Using a variety of finger rolls, a fallaway jumper and his patented "dipper dunk," Chamberlain scored 2707 points, for an unheard of 37.7 average. He also grabbed 1941 rebounds, for a 27.0 average, compared to Russell's 1778 and 24.0.

But it was the Celtics, compiling a 59-16 mark, ten games

OPPOSITE: *George Yardley, the Detroit Pistons' "Bald Eagle," drives for two against the Knicks in 1957 game action. Yardley was just 6-5 and weighed only 195, but he could play at the offensive end. In 1957-8, Yardley not only led the NBA in scoring with a 27.8 average, but he also became the first player to score more than 2000 points in a season. The Bald Eagle hit for 2001.*

RIGHT: *This was the big battle of the late 1950s and most of the 1960s. When Bill Russell (right) and the Celtics met Wilt Chamberlain and the Warriors, the sparks were sure to fly. The two giants battled tooth and nail under the basket. Though Wilt usually won the battle of individual statistics, it was Russell who often won the war, since the Celtics won the majority of the games. And while the two great centers had distinctly different styles, they were probably the two greatest rebounders the game has ever known.*

LEFT: *It's a typical Celtics-Hawks battle in March of 1960. This one was played at the Boston Garden. St Louis' Cliff Hagan battles with Boston's Gene Conley underneath. Looking on are Bob Pettit (9) and Frank Ramsey (23). Conley, incidentally, was a 6-8 backup center for the Celtics during the winter, but in the summer he played as a pitcher for the Milwaukee Braves.*

BELOW: *It's Chamberlain vs Russell again, this time in November of 1959. Watching the two big men go at it are Woody Sauldsberry (14) and Tom Heinsohn (15). When it was over the Celtics were on top, 115-106, and Coach Red Auerbach was lighting another victory cigar.*

OPPOSITE: *This time it's Russell hooking over Clyde Lovellette of the Hawks. This one was in the seventh game of the NBA championship series in 1960, and the Celtics won yet another, 122-103.*

better than the Warriors' 49-26, who were clearly the superior team. And while Chamberlain sometimes won the individual battle with Russell, it was Boston that won the wars. The Celts were more powerful than ever, having added Bill Russell's college teammate, K C Jones, a superb defensive guard. With this combination, Boston topped Philadelphia in six games during the playoff semi-finals, then went on to win still another title by whipping Bob Pettit and the St Louis Hawks in yet another seven-game finale.

Even then, the Celtics were often at their best when the chips were down, when everything was on the line. They rarely lost a big game, and even during the regular season, when many teams often let down, if only for a week or two, Boston was always up. One of the Celtic players once explained the team's incredible competitiveness by saying, "We hated to lose two games in a row. When we did lose one, the next game was always like the championship."

As the 1960-61 season got underway all the individual achievements seemed to fall to the many new stars who were coming into the league. In fact, the NBA had now become a coast-to-coast operation with the transfer of the once-proud Minneapolis franchise to Los Angeles. It would turn out to be a good move: The Los Angeles Lakers would soon become a flagship franchise for the NBA.

It was still the Celtics, however, who won the most games, finishing the regular season with a 57-22 log. Yet look at the scoring leaders and Celtics are hard to find. Chamberlain was again on top, with a 38.4 average and 3033 points. Baylor was next, with 2538 points and a 34.8 average. In third place was a sensational rookie, Oscar Robertson, who

had completed a brilliant career at the University of Cincinnati. Now he was with the Cincinnati Royals, and he was already one of the great all-around players in the league. He averaged 30.5 points a game as a rookie and led the league with 9.7 assists per game.

The rest of the scoring race was a combination of old and new. Following the Big O was Pettit, then Jack Twyman, veteran Dolph Schayes, New York's Willie Naulls, the veteran Arizin, then Bailey Howell and Gene Shue of Detroit, guard Richie Guerin of New York, Hagan of St Louis and finally Tom Heinsohn, the first Celtic on the list. Several notches below Heinsohn was another highly-touted rookie, Jerry West of West Virginia and the L A Lakers, who, along with Robertson, would quickly become one of the greatest guards the game has ever known.

But despite all the greatness in the league, it was still the Celtics again in the playoffs. Red Auerbach had added six-foot, six-inch forward Tom "Satch" Sanders, another superb defensive player, to strengthen the team even more, and the club whipped both Syracuse and St Louis in five games to wrap up what seemed to be their annual NBA title. Once again the word "dynasty" was beginning to appear in the basketball press.

A year later, the Celtics were even better, and so was Wilt Chamberlain. Though the Big Dipper was, in the minds of some, already falling under the shadow of Bill Russell as a team player and a winner (Chamberlain would usually "outstatistic" Russell in their head to head meetings, but Boston would generally win the game), he was also proving the most awesome offensive force the game had ever seen. It

OPPOSITE: *Forward Elgin Baylor and guard Jerry West gave the Los Angeles Lakers one of the best one-two punches in the game. In this 1962 playoff game against Detroit Baylor grabs a rebound as West (44) turns to head up court. The other Laker is Frank Selvy (11).*

was amazing enough that he had come into the league and averaged well over 30 points a game. But what he did in the 1961-62 season was simply incredible, an 80-game performance that will never be matched again. For over those 80 games Wilt Chamberlain scored 4029 points, an average of 50.4 points a game!

Think about it. It's a rarity for most college and pro players even to score 50 points in a single game anytime during their careers. Chamberlain averaged 50 points over a gruelling, 80-game schedule, often playing 48 minutes a

night and being pushed and shoved, grabbed and pulled, by opposing forwards and centers who tried everything to stop him. Yet in spite of this, Wilt scored 60 or more points 15 times and went over the 50 point mark some 44 times.

It was also a year in which Laker stars Elgin Baylor and Jerry West each had games of 63 points. And on another occasion Baylor threw in 61. In fact, Baylor's 63-point game came early in the year, when the Lakers were playing the Warriors. It was a triple overtime game, and that same night Chamberlain merely scored 78.

Then came the night of 2 March 1962. The Warriors were hosting the New York Knickerbockers at a neutral court in Hershey, Pennsylvania. In the first period, Wilt scored 23 of his team's 42 points. The Knicks had 26, but led by Willie Naulls, Cleveland Buckner and Richie Guerin, they stormed back to score 42 points of their own in the second. But Philly still led at the half 79-68. And Wilt had 41 points. He seemed on his way to yet another big night. The question was, how big?

With the Knicks still scoring and threatening to turn the game around, Wilt kept shooting, and now his teammates were feeding him underneath. He nailed 28 more in the third period to run his total to 69 points. His record of 78, set earlier in the year, now seemed destined to fall. And not only was Wilt hitting on his fallaway jumper and dunks, he was also connecting on most of his free throws, which was unusual, because throughout his long NBA career Wilt Chamberlain was a notoriously bad free-throw shooter.

In the fourth quarter it seemed that everything he threw up went in. And when the Knicks fouled him he continued to make the charity tosses as well. With eight minutes left, he already had 79 points. Then he was up over 90. Everyone watching had the same thought in mind: Could he make it 100?

With just 46 seconds left the big guy took a lob pass close to the hoop and stuffed it home. It was his 100th point of the game and put the cap on a Philadelphia 169-147 victory, the most points scored by two NBA teams in the history of the game. Wilt had hit on 36 of 63 field goal tries and 28 of 32 free throws. He also found time to grab 25 rebounds in one of the most exciting basketball performances of all time.

ABOVE: *Though the Lakers often challenged the Celtics for the NBA crown, they always came up short. Here Boston's Bob Cousy goes between West and Baylor, but the difference between the two teams was usually the play of Bill Russell.*

OPPOSITE: *Guard Sam Jones (24) was still another of the great players discoverd by Red Auerbach during the Celtics dynasty years. Jones was a superb scorer who often produced in clutch situations.*

But come playoff time it was the Celtics again. Boston had finished the regular season with a 60-20 record, then whipped Philadelphia and Wilt in the semi-finals, winning the seventh and deciding game 109-107. In the final round against Los Angeles, the Celts were again extended to a full seven games. In fact, they had to win game six to force a seventh. And that one went into overtime when the Lakers Frank Selvy missed a short jumper that could have won it for LA in regulation. But in the overtime Boston did it again, winning the game, 110-107. They just didn't lose the close ones.

It was the Celts' fourth consecutive championship, a new NBA record. Bill Sharman had retired before the season, but Sam Jones stepped in to average 18.4 points a game. And even with Cousy getting older the team rolled on. Russell was as good as ever, and the system put in by Red Auerbach produced winners. With all the incredible talent in the league now — the Chamberlains, Baylors, Robertsons, Wests, Pettits — no team could beat the Celtics. They just kept rolling.

And it stayed that way for four more seasons. Chicago came into the league in 1961-62, and a year later the Philadelphia franchise, with Wilt Chamberlain, moved to San Francisco, giving the West Coast a second professional team. Wilt would average 44.8 points a game his first year in San Francisco, but the Celtics would add a six-foot, five-inch rookie from Ohio State, John Havlicek, as well as veteran reserve center Clyde Lovellette. As a team they were better than ever, and the opposition continued to fall.

In 1962-63 they took the title by whipping the Lakers in six games. After the season the great Bob Cousy retired, but the Celtics didn't miss a beat. In the championship round in 1964 they soundly trounced Wilt and the San Francisco Warriors in five games. A year later, 1965, they took the Lakers in five games. They were, without a doubt, the greatest team pro basketball had ever seen.

Philadelphia was back in the league again, the Syracuse franchise having moved to the City of Brotherly Love. The new Philly team was called the 76ers, and in 1964-65 they re-acquired Wilt from San Francisco. But not even that stopped the Boston steamroller.

Even though Tom Heinsohn had retired prior to the 1965-66 season and Philly had gone on to beat out the Celts for the Eastern Division title by a single game, come playoff time the Celtics were ready. They eliminated the 76ers in just five games and then defeated the Lakers once again, this time in seven tough games. It was their eighth consecutive championship and their ninth in ten years.

It was also a year in which more new names were making themselves heard in the NBA. San Francisco had a hotshot rookie forward, Rick Barry from Miami, while Nate Thurmond in San Francisco and Willis Reed in New York were a pair of rugged centers making their presence felt. Jerry Lucas was established in Cincinnati, playing alongside the Big O. Center Zelmo Beaty and guard Lenny Wilkins had replaced the retired Bob Pettit to take over in St Louis.

And in Boston, Red Auerbach announced his retirement as coach, though he would remain with the club as general

LEFT: *One of the brightest new names to emerge in the 1965-6 season was that of San Francisco center Nate Thurmond (42). Looking as if he were going to bite him is Cincinnati's Wayne Embry (15).*

OPPOSITE: *Rookie Rick Barry of San Francisco in action during the 1965-6 season. Barry averaged 25.7 points his first year, 35.6 the next season. The 6-7 forward from Miami was one of the great scorers in NBA history.*

manager and later as president. The new coach was none other than Bill Russell, who would also continue playing and try to lead the Celtics to a ninth straight title.

But 1966-67 turned out to be the year of Wilt Chamberlain and the Philadelphia 76ers. It was a year in which Wilt concentrated more on passing and defense, scoring only when he had to, and with a fine supporting cast led by forwards Chet Walker, Billy Cunningham and Luke Jackson, and by guards Hal Greer, Larry Costello and Wally Jones, the 76ers finished the regular season with an amazing 68-13

record. Boston, still a powerhouse, wasn't far behind at 60-21. These two were clearly the best teams in the league.

The two giants clashed in the semi-finals of the playoffs, and Philly at last overcame the Celtics in five games. From there Philly went on to defeat San Francisco four games to two for the title. It was the first year since he had come into the league that Wilt was not the NBA scoring champion. But he gladly traded that honor for the championship, hoping to end the talk that he was not a winner by finally stepping out from the winning shadow of Bill Russell.

OPPOSITE: *Two of the best guards of the 1960s go head to head, as Philadelphia's Hal Greer drives on Jerry West of the Lakers. Greer had more than 21,500 points during his career, while Jerry West had more than 25,000.*

RIGHT: *"Red" Auerbach, the most successful coach in NBA history. He piloted the Celtics to a slew of NBA titles, then became general manager and finally president of the team. Possessor of one of the shrewdest minds in the sport, Auerbach would often infuriate opponents by lighting a victory cigar on the bench as soon as he felt his club had the game won.*

But the Celtic dynasty wasn't done yet. Perhaps what they achieved in the next two seasons was more incredible than all the previous titles, for the team was aging rapidly. Russell was 34, Sam Jones 35, forward Bailey Howell, acquired in a trade, 31. John Havlicek, at 28, had become the new floor leader, though the club still depended heavily on what Russell gave them underneath. In 1967-68 they finished at 54-28, eight games behind the 76ers. Then came the playoffs.

Once again the Celtics rose to the occasion. Trailing the 76ers three games to one in the Eastern finals, the Celts rallied to win three straight. In the finals they again whipped the Lakers, 4-2, for their tenth title in 12 seasons. But how long could it continue? A year later it seemed to end, for Boston finished the regular season in fourth place, trailing Baltimore, Philadelphia and the New York Knicks. The balance of power seemed to be changing.

Wilt Chamberlain had been traded to the LA Lakers in the offseason, and his presence in a lineup that already had Elgin Baylor and Jerry West seemed to make the Lakers unbeatable. After the Celtics eliminated the 76ers in five games and the New York Knicks in six, they found themselves going up against this new Laker combination for the championship. Could the old men summon up one more great effort?

Somehow, someway, they did it. The Lakers extended the Celts to seven games, but in the finale Boston once again called upon all those years of Celtics magic and won it by a scant two points, 108-106, for their 11th title in 13 years, perhaps the greatest one of all. Right after the season Bill Russell announced his retirement, and he was followed quickly by Sam Jones. It was the end of an era, the era of the Boston Celtics, an era that had seen one team dominate an entire league in a way that would never be possible again.

BIGGER, BETTER, STRONGER, FASTER

The end of the Celtics era by no means placed a halt to the progress of professional basketball. The game was firmly established now, and more finished and complete players were coming into the league every year. Indeed, there were so many good players entering the professional ranks that a new league, the American Basketball Association, was formed and began play during the 1967-68 season. Though many ABA players were considered second-line pros, the new league did sign some blue-chippers and lasted until a merger was completed in 1976-77.

As for the NBA, Bill Russell's retirement might have ended an era, but the young players coming in were about to put their own stamp on the pro game. Even when the Celts had won their 11th title in 1968-69, the composition of the league was already changing. For example, the leading scorer that year was rookie Elvin Hayes of the new San Diego franchise. The Big E had been a college star at Houston and had come into the pros without missing a beat. He was also the league's fourth best rebounder. But perhaps an even more surprising rookie was six-foot, eight-inch Westley Unseld of Louisville, who used his great strength and quickness to transform the Baltimore Bullets into a first-place team. Short for a center, Unseld nevertheless finished behind Wilt in the rebounding race and was good enough to be named both Rookie of the Year and Most Valuable Player.

Baltimore also had a young guard named Earl "The Pearl" Monroe, whose slippery moves made him one of the great one-on-one offensive players in the game. Other young stars were guards Gail Goodrich of Phoenix, Dave Bing of Detroit and Walt Frazier of the New York Knicks. Frazier, known by the nickname Clyde, was a magnificent defensive player whose fast hands led to many a steal and subsequent fast break.

Jeff Mullins of San Francisco, Lou Hudson of Atlanta and Dave DeBusschere of New York were other young players making their marks. And the Knicks also had a pair of heralded collegians splitting time at small forward. They were muscular Cazzie Russell of Michigan and Bill Bradley from Princeton, who had taken time off to study at Oxford as a Rhodes Scholar but was now back.

In fact, with Frazier, Bradley, Russell and DeBusschere joined by center Willis Reed and wiley guard Dick Barnett, the Knicks entered the 1969-70 season with an improving ballclub that played an unselfish team game in a system molded by coach Red Holzman. The powerful Reed was the anchor at center, but the club played together with a cohesiveness that enabled them to beat teams that may have been physically superior.

BELOW LEFT: *Elvin Hayes entered the NBA in 1968 and averaged 28.4 points a game as a rookie. Here, he shoots over Wilt Chamberlain, with Jerry West looking on.*

BELOW RIGHT: *Rookie of the year and MVP in 1968-69: Bullet Wes Unseld.*

OPPOSITE: *Cazzie Russell (33) of the Knicks was an explosive scorer.*

ABOVE: *Lew Alcindor of UCLA joined the Milwaukee Bucks in 1969-70 and became an instant superstar. A year later the 7-2 center led the Bucks to an NBA title. He soon changed his name to Kareem Abdul-Jabbar, but his game stayed the same. He is now the NBA's all-time leading scorer, and he has won several more championships with the Los Angeles Lakers.*

RIGHT: *Rugged Willis Reed (19) was always one of the NBA's hardest-working players. At 6-9, Reed often had to go up against taller men, but he could play inside with anyone and helped the New York Knicks to a pair of NBA titles.*

There were 14 teams in the NBA as the new season started. The league had been growing steadily and now had franchises in Milwaukee, Atlanta (the Hawks had moved from St Louis), Phoenix, Seattle and San Diego. It had truly become a nationwide enterprise. And there was still another super rookie joining the league in 1969-70. He was Lew Alcindor, the seven-foot, two-inch center from UCLA, who had just completed a brilliant college career. Stepping into the pros without losing effectiveness, Alcindor transformed the Milwaukee Bucks into an immediate contender, and they chased the Knicks all year.

But it was a New York season. The Knicks came out of the gate like gangbusters, winning 23 of their first 24 games, including a then-record 18 in a row. Great scoring balance, teamwork and defense were the team trademarks, and sell-out crowds at Madison Square Garden screamed in anticipation of the old franchise's first NBA title. The team won

the East with a 60-22 mark, finishing just four games ahead of the Alcindor-led Milwaukee Bucks. Now came the playoffs, the first playoffs that didn't include the Boston Celtics since 1950.

The Knicks were tested in the first round and had to go the full seven games before defeating the Bullets. But then they disposed of Milwaukee and rookie Alcindor in just five. That set up the championship confrontation with the Los Angeles Lakers, a team that had Wilt Chamberlain back in the lineup. (Wilt had missed most of the regular season with a knee injury.)

After four games the two teams were deadlocked. Then, in game five, though Willis Reed went down with a serious leg injury, the Knicks held on to win. Without Reed in game six, however, the Lakers won easily. Now, with the seventh and deciding game about to be played, Reed's availability became the big question. The rugged center from Gram-

TOP LEFT: *Cool Walt Frazier ran the Knicks backcourt during their title years.*

ABOVE: *Charlie Scott of the Phoenix Suns could run and score with anyone.*

RIGHT: *The one and only Oscar Robertson helped the Bucks to an NBA title.*

bling didn't take pre-game warmups, but when he appeared on the court the huge crowd at Madison Square Garden raised the roof. Limping noticeably and obviously not 100 percent, Reed hit his first two jumpshots of the game. It was enough to inspire his teammates, and the Knicks went on to win the game and the championship 113-99.

But neither the Knicks nor anyone else was about to establish the kind of dominance the Celtics had shown for so long. The 1970s would be a decade of great players and many different champion teams. That was probably the best thing that could have happened to the NBA. The league stretched east to west, north to south, and with a good number of teams in the hunt, fan interest was increasing.

In 1970-71 the 17 teams were broken up into four divisions. Operating out of the Midwest, Milwaukee compiled a 66-16 mark to enter the playoffs as favorites. The Bucks had added the great veteran Oscar Robertson who, at the

age of 32, had never won an NBA title. His job was to be a settling influence on the young Bucks, and that's what he was. Milwaukee won it all, losing only two games in three seven-game series. And in the finals they whipped the Baltimore Bullets in four straight.

It was also a year of outstanding rookies, as centers Dave Cowens of Boston and Bob Lanier of Detroit entered the league, along with guards Pete Maravich of Atlanta and Calvin Murphy of San Diego. The rival ABA, still struggling for respectability, had landed big Dan Issel of Kentucky and Charlie Scott of North Carolina. However, some ABA stars were returning to the NBA. Connie Hawkins had joined Phoenix earlier, and now 1968 Olympic hero Spencer Haywood joined Seattle of the NBA.

The 1971 season also marked the 25th anniversary of the league, and to commemorate the occasion, the NBA picked a silver anniversary team, composed of the ten best retired

players in league history. The team was made up of Bill Russell and George Mikan at center, Bob Pettit, Dolph Schayes, Paul Arizin and Joe Fulks at forward, and Bob Cousy, Bill Sharman, Bob Davies and Sam Jones at guard. It was an impressive unit, to be sure, but many would argue that plenty of the present NBA players would be ready to challenge for spots once their careers ended.

The 1971-72 season turned out to be the year of the Lakers. At long last the Lakers took the NBA title — or at least the first time since the franchise had moved from Minneapolis. With a starting unit of Jerry West and Gail Goodrich at guards, Wilt Chamberlain at center and Happy Hairston and Jim McMillian at forwards, the Lakers were a record-setting quintet. They set a record with their 69-13 regular season record, as well as an incredible, 33-game winning streak. They also set a mark when they walloped the Warriors 169-99, the greatest victory margin for a single game

in league history. The team was so good that the finals were a 4-1 romp over the New York Knicks.

One other note. Before the season had started, Lew Alcindor legally changed his name to Kareem Abdul-Jabbar as part of his conversion to the Muslim religion.

OPPOSITE: *Kareem Adbul-Jabbar holds the ball high over his head as he looks for a Milwaukee teammate. Whether playing for the Bucks or Lakers, the big guy was always the center of interest. Abdul-Jabbar's "sky hook" is perhaps the most unstoppable shot in basketball history.*

BELOW: *Even in his twilight years Wilt Chamberlain was still an imposing physical force. In 1972 he didn't score the way he used to, concentrating more on defense. He still led the league in rebounding and the result was an NBA title for the Lakers.*

A year later, the Knicks were back, taking a second NBA crown in four years. The nucleus of Willis Reed, Walt Frazier, Dave DeBusschere and Bill Bradley were all veterans and still playing great team ball. Earl Monroe had come over from Baltimore and had teamed with Frazier to form one of the best backcourts in the league. Veteran Jerry Lucas could fill in at center or forward, while Phil Jackson, Dean Meminger and Henry Bibby all contributed to the effort.

Injuries may have helped the Knicks in the playoffs. Against Boston, which had finished at 68-14 in the regular season, the Knicks were helped by an arm injury to John Havlicek. And in the finals against the Lakers, Jerry West wasn't playing at full strength. For whatever reasons, the Knicks won, and their team game was still a thing to behold.

The continuing changing face of the league could be seen by the top individual players. Guard Nate "Tiny" Archibald

of the Kansas City-Omaha Kings (the old Cincinnati Royals franchise) won both the scoring and assists titles. Center Bob McAdoo of Buffalo (another new franchise) was the Rookie of the Year, while hustling Dave Cowens, the Celtics' center, was the Most Valuable Player.

The end of the 1973 season also marked the end of still another great career. Wilt Chamberlain retired. The big guy had become more of a team player, a cog in the wheel in his final years. He averaged just 13.2 points his last season, but he was still enough of a force inside at age 36 to lead the league in rebounds, with 18.2 a game. He retired with a 30.1 career scoring average, the best ever, and a then-record 31,419 points, a mark since topped by Abdul-Jabbar.

But the more things change the more they remain the same. In 1973-74 Boston regained the NBA championship by defeating Milwaukee in seven games. Led by Dave Cowens, John Havlicek, Jo Jo White and Paul Silas, the Celtics were still a running, hustling, fastbreaking team, with

LEFT: *Rugged Paul Silas espoused a work ethic second to none, and at 6-7, he loved to bang inside. The Celtics were one of several teams for which he played.*

BELOW: *Boston's Dave Cowens didn't have the talents of a Bill Russell. But he was such a hard-worker that the results were nearly the same.*

OPPOSITE: *Ohio State's Jerry Lucas was as great a pro as he was a collegian. Though just 6-8, his perfect sense of timing enabled him to rebound against the likes of Russell and Chamberlain. He was also an unselfish player, who could fit in anywhere, an all-pro and a winner.*

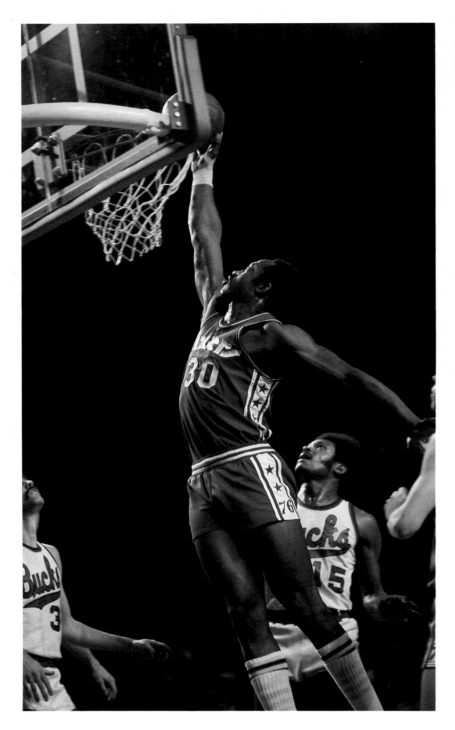

the same kind of pride that had spurred the club in the Cousy-Russell era. They wouldn't dominate as they once did, but they remained one of the best teams in the league.

A year later still another new champion arrived. The Golden State Warriors (nee the San Francisco Warriors) took the title behind the shooting of Rick Barry and a cast of virtual unknowns. Keith Wilkes from UCLA became a key contributor as a rookie, while defensive center Clifford Ray kept control of things in the middle and guard Phil Smith provided some additional offensive power. But mostly it was a case of a team peaking at the right time. Boston, Washington and Buffalo all had better regular season records than the Warriors, but they knocked each other off in the playoffs, and then Golden State shocked the Bullets by defeating them in four straight.

It was also a year that saw three more greats of the game hang up their sneakers. Oscar Robertson, Jerry West and Willis Reed had all called it quits before the season began. But a rookie who had everyone waiting in anticipation was Bill Walton, the great center from UCLA. Walton had joined the Portland Trail Blazers, hoping to do for them what he had done for the Bruins. But the big redhead injured a foot and played just 35 games. His time was yet to come.

Golden State had the best record in 1975-76, justifying their title of a year earlier. But they were upset by Phoenix in the playoffs, and Boston came on to win still another title. The Celts whipped the Suns in six games for cham-

pionship number 13 – hardly an unlucky number for Boston.

But the big news was the jumping of players from the rival ABA, which seemed on the verge of folding. The biggest signing was of forward George McGinnis, who left Indiana and signed with the 76ers. And in another major player move, Milwaukee traded Kareem Abdul-Jabbar to the LA Lakers, making LA a powerhouse team once again.

A year later the leagues merged. It was inevitable, since the bidding war had driven salaries sky high, and the ABA, although lasting nine years, just couldn't compete. The result was the NBA taking over four ABA franchises intact. The new teams were the Denver Nuggets, the Indiana Pacers, the San Antonio Spurs and the New York Nets.

Some of the outstanding players moving into the NBA were David Thompson and Dan Issel of Denver, Billy Knight of Indiana, George Gervin and Larry Kenon of San Antonio. There was one other. He had played for the New York Nets, but after the merger the Nets refused to renegotiate his contract, and he was moved to the Philadelphia 76ers before the 1976-77 season began. To many, this player was the most exciting in all of basketball, a major talent that not even the ABA could hide. His name was Julius Erving, the six-foot seven-inch forward known everywhere as Doctor J.

There were now 22 teams in the NBA, a far cry from the eight franchieses that helped solidify the league just a little over a decade earlier. There were four divisions, with

OPPOSITE FAR LEFT: *Big George McGinnis was a star in both the ABA and NBA during the 1970s. At 6-8, he was one of the strongest players in basketball, a top scorer and rebounder.*

OPPOSITE LEFT: *Injuries have prevented Bill Walton from duplicating his college success in the pros. But when healthy the center is as good as they come. In 1977 he led the Portland Trailblazers to an NBA championship.*

RIGHT: *The electrifying Julius Erving in motion for the Philadelphia 76ers. Dr J, as he was called, began his career with the New York Nets of the ABA and quickly showed he was one of the most amazing one-on-one players ever. With the Sixers the Doc proved to everyone that he was an all-around superstar and future Hall of Famer.*

heated competition in each one. With Erving and McGinnis in the lineup, the 76ers won the East with a 50-32 mark. Houston topped the Central by a game over Washington. ABA refugee Denver surprised everyone in the Midwest with a 50-32 mark, while the Lakers and Abdul-Jabbar won the West with the best record in the league at 53-29. But just four games behind the Lakers were the surprising Portland Trailblazers.

With Bill Walton healthy enough to play in 65 games, the Blazers had become a contender. Walton was doing the same things he did at UCLA, scoring when he had to, playing great defense and rebounding. He was also one of the best passing centers ever to play the game. Combining with power forward Maurice Lucas and guard Lionel Hollins to form a tough nucleus, Walton led the league in rebounding, with a 14.4 average, and also led in blocked shots, with 3.25 a game.

But it wasn't until the Blazers shocked the LA Lakers in four straight during the semi-finals of the playoffs that people realized that the new Walton gang was a team to be reckoned with. Then, in the finals, the Blazers went up against Julius Erving and the 76ers. When Philly won the first two games it looked as if the upstart Blazers had finally met their match. But Walton and the Blazers then came back to life. With the big redhead triggering a controlled fastbreak, just as he had at UCLA, the Blazers went on to take four straight and win their first NBA championship.

Once again the unpredictable had happened.

The all-league team for 1977 showed a combination of old and new. Abdul-Jabbar and Elvin Hayes were the old, while scoring champ Pete Maravich, David Thompson and Paul Westphal were the new. Adrian Dantley from Notre Dame was the top rookie.

It looked like more of the same the next season. Portland started out as if they were the class of the league, with Bill Walton on his way to becoming the super center everyone had thought he would be. But the team was hit by injuries, Walton himself being sidelined the last two months. The big guy would play only 14 games over the next four seasons, a brilliant career sabotaged by bad feet. But he was still good enough in 58 games to be named the league's Most Valuable Player.

And the Washington Bullets (the franchise had moved from Baltimore) were good enough to become NBA champs, defeating another surprise team, the Seattle Supersonics, in seven games. Led by the veteran combination of Elvin Hayes and Wes Unseld, the Bullets were another club that peaked at the right time, defeating tough Philly in the semi-finals before whipping Seattle to take the crown.

Then, as the decade came to an end, there was still another champion. The 1977-78 runner-up Seattle Supersonics returned a year later to win the 1978-79 crown. Only the defending champion Washington Bullets had a better regular season mark than Coach Len Wilkins' Sonics. The

Sonics certainly weren't a super team in the classic sense. They were led by a pair of outstanding guards in Gus Williams and Dennis Johnson, though neither could be considered an Oscar Robertson or Jerry West. Young Jack Sikma was a good, rugged center, but no Russell or Abdul-Jabbar. John Johnson and Lonnie Shelton were the forwards, but no one would accuse either of them of being an Elgin Baylor or Julius Erving. Yet the Sonics jelled and defeated the Bullets in the finals to take the title. There was jubilation in the streets of Seattle, but as the decade came to an end there was some concern in other circles.

Though the league seemed balanced and competitive, with no team able to repeat as champions in 11 years, there was growing worry about the popularity of the pro game. Television ratings were down, and many people seemed to feel the games had become somewhat routine. There was a

feeling that many players no longer played up to their capacity game after game. Comfortable with long-term, million-dollar contracts, the players were content to go at a relaxed pace until playoff time. With so many teams making the playoffs, why bust a gut for that extra rebound or basket when it really didn't mean anything?

Another reason for the loss of popularity might have been the demise of the big city franchises. The Knicks, Celtics, Chicago Bulls, even the Lakers, had not been contenders for several years, and those big-city markets were always important for the ultimate success of the league. Even the Celtics were nowhere. The once-dominant franchise compiled records of just 32-50 in 1978 and 29-53 in 1979, the latter putting them dead last in the Eastern Division.

Another reason might have been a lack of recognizable superstars. The scoring leader during the past three sea-

LEFT: *Jack Sikma is a fine example of a role-playing center who can help make the right team a champion, as he did with the 1978-9 Seattle Supersonics. Sikma averaged 15.6 points and 12.4 rebounds. More important, however, was the way he fit in with Coach Len Wilkins' team concept. Sometimes – often – that's all it takes.*

OPPOSITE: *Slender George Gervin was known as the Ice Man for the cool way he played the game. The 6-7 guard played with Virginia and San Antonio of the ABA and came into the NBA when the Spurs were admitted in 1976. No matter where he played, he was a scoring champion with icewater in his veins.*

sons had been George Gervin, an ABA refugee who came into the NBA with the San Antonio Spurs. The rebounding leader in 1978 was Truck Robinson of New Orleans. Kevin Porter of New Jersey led the league in assists. These weren't exactly household names. Though they were multi-talented performers, they just didn't seem to have the charisma of the previous generation, the Wests, Robertsons, Fraziers, Monroes, Chamberlains, Havliceks and Reeds.

Yet on the whole, the players continued to have great natural talent. They were bigger and better, stronger and

faster than the players of 15 years earlier. But were they the same kind of competitors? Did they have the same kind of drive? Some said no, the contracts were too fat.

The league was still pondering these questions as the 1979-80 season got underway. And while no one might have realized it at the time, many of the league's problems were about to be solved by the simple addition of two incredible rookies going to a pair of the league's glamour teams. They had been linked as collegians, and they were destined to be linked together once more as professionals.

Larry Bird was a six-foot, nine-inch forward from Indiana State University. As a collegian, he was so good that he took an unheralded team to the finals of the NCAA tournament his senior year. Red Auerbach, the wiley president and general manager of the Boston Celtics, saw the potential and drafted him a year early, when Bird's original class was due to graduate. The year's wait would turn out to be more than worth it, for Bird would be the man to restore the Celtics to their former glory.

The other rookie was Earvin "Magic" Johnson of Michigan State, a six-foot, nine-inch point guard. Johnson left Michigan after his sophomore season, but he had already led the Spartans to the national championship, his team defeating Bird and Indiana State for the title. He was drafted by the LA Lakers, where he would be playing alongside the already legendary Kareem Abdul-Jabbar.

Just why were these two rookies so special? They were both complete players, all-around performers who could do everything on the court. And they were leaders, the kind of players who wanted the ball at crunch time, were willing to take the crucial shot. They dared to be great and to take the chance of failure that went with it.

OPPOSITE: *There are many who already call Boston's Larry Bird the best ever. Bird came into the NBA after a story-book career at Indiana State and simply keeps on getting better. His game seems to know no weakness. He is the consummate team player, with all the individual skills, enabling him to score, rebound and throw incredible passes. He has led the Celts to several NBA titles and has won a slew of individual awards. He's simply a once-in-a-lifetime player.*

RIGHT: *The other player of the 1980s is Earvin "Magic" Johnson of the L A Lakers. Magic was often compared with Larry Bird in college and the two are still being compared as pros. Like Bird, the Magic man can do it all, and he also has a number of NBA titles to show for his efforts. At 6-9, he is a point guard who can handle the ball as well as anyone. Add to that scoring and rebounding skills, and you have the complete player.*

brilliant again, and while Julius Erving of the 76ers took the league's MVP prize, fans in Boston thanked Larry Bird for helping to put yet another championship banner on the rafters of old Boston Garden.

So the pattern of the 1980s was established. It would be Boston and the Lakers, Bird and Magic, Kareem and Parish and McHale, plus the players who were to follow. These would be the two teams battling for the championship. But with one important exception. The Lakers, with Magic recovered from the knee injury, took the title again in 1981-82, but the following year the Philadelphia 76ers decided to go for it all.

Tired of playing second fiddle to the Cadillac teams of the league, the Sixers went out and got the man they wanted, center Moses Malone from Houston. Malone was a six-foot, ten-inch rebounder who was a terror off the offensive backboard. He was a tireless worker inside and wore down opponents with his tenacity. So good was he that he had already been named the league's Most Valuable Player twice, in 1978-79 and again in 1981-82.

OPPOSITE: *Magic Johnson moving underneath to rebound and looking more like a big center than a point guard.*

LEFT: *Jamaal Wilkes, who played with some of the great UCLA teams in college, also played with some top Laker teams as a pro.*

BOTTOM: *As competitive a player as anyone who has played the game, the 6-9 Bird is the annual winner of the NBA's long-range shooting contest during the All-Star break. You say big men don't shoot well from the outside? Well, someone forgot to tell Larry Bird.*

Bird could do just about everything from his forward spot. He wasn't afraid to mix it up underneath, was an outstanding passer for a big man and could shoot from in close or from far out. Johnson was a basketball phenomenon, a six-foot, nine-inch player who could handle the ball as well as anyone. He, too, was an outstanding passer, a completely unselfish player whose enthusiastic personality and quick smile was infectious.

Both Bird and Johnson had brilliant rookie seasons. Bird played in all 82 games for the Celtics, scored 1745 points for a 21.3 average, grabbed 852 rebounds and dished out 370 assists. He brought the Celts back to respectability, and within a year he would be ready to lead them back to the pinnacle. But in 1979-80 he was simply the NBA's Rookie of the Year. Magic did even better. He took over the floor leadership of the Lakers from day one. Not only did he average 18 points a game, but he still found time to hand off for 563 assists and grab 596 rebounds. Because of his all-around play, NBA followers would coin a new term, the "triple-double," meaning a player was in double figures in scoring, assists and rebounds. Magic Johnson would do it routinely.

But what was even more special about Magic's rookie year was that the team won the Western Division with a 60-22 record and went on from there to take the NBA title. He had been the missing piece on a team that already included Kareem and forward Jamaal (formerly Keith) Wilkes.

A year later Magic showed just how important he was to the Lakers. He was limited to just 37 games by a knee injury, and the Lakers fell from contention. But when Larry Bird was joined in Boston by seven-foot Robert Parish at center and a six-foot, ten-inch rookie named Kevin McHale at forward, the Celtics had a front line that blew people away. The team had a 62-20 record in the regular season and went on to reclaim the championship. Bird was

With Malone complementing Julius Erving, and with point guard Maurice Cheeks and shooting guard Andrew Toney, the Sixers became the scourge of the league. They were 65-17 in the regular season, and come the playoffs Malone brashly predicted that the Sixers would go "four, four and four," meaning they would not lose a single game.

He was almost right. They lost only once en route to the NBA title. For Malone, it meant a third MVP, and for Doctor J, who had been so great for so long, it was that elusive NBA title he had sought for so long. No one likes to see a great player in any sport toil for years without ever once grabbing the gold ring. Thanks to Moses Malone and the rest of the Sixers, including the good Doctor, it was theirs.

But the next four seasons found the old pattern repeated — Boston, Los Angeles, Boston, Los Angeles. They were the best and invariably one of them would win. After Malone took the MVP in 1982-83, Larry Bird would win it for three consecutive years. And when that string was finally broken in 1986-87, it was Earvin "Magic" Johnson who took the top prize.

While it was Larry Bird and Magic Johnson who perhaps put the personality back into the league, others followed, as more outstanding college ballplayers turned pro and put their own stamp of greatness on the National Basketball Association. And no matter where these players went, they attracted new fans, so great was their level of skill.

The names of the 1980s read like a basketball who's who, and all these players have made their presence felt and are still doing it. Bernard King, Sidney Moncrief, Mark Aguirre, Darrell Griffith, Danny Ainge, Ralph Sampson, Isiah Thomas, Terry Cummings, James Worthy, Eric Floyd, Dominique Wilkins, Michael Jordan, Charles Barkley, Clyde Drexler, Patrick Ewing, Akeem Olajuwon, Ron Harper, Buck Williams and Chuck Person.

There are others, of course, but these are just some of the impact players from around the league, players who cer-

OPPOSITE TOP LEFT: *Moses Malone became a pro right out of high school in 1974. Since that time, the 6-10 center has become the best offensive rebounder the game has ever known. He has also been a Most Valuable Player and has helped lead the Philadelphia 76ers to an NBA crown.*

OPPOSITE TOP RIGHT: *Two of the best going head to head: Philly's Julius Erving pops a jumper over Milwaukee's Marques Johnson. The Doc is considered the best of his time, but a Marques Johnson is also a bona fide all-star who can take control of a game.*

OPPOSITE BOTTOM: *One of the bright new superstars of the mid-1980s is Mark Aguirre of the Dallas Mavericks. Aguirre was an All-American as a freshman at DePaul and has played at that All-star level ever since. As the expansionist Mavericks slowly become one of the NBA's better teams, the offense continues to center around Aguirre.*

RIGHT: *Magic Johnson lofts one toward the hoop. With aging center Kareem Abdul-Jabbar playing a lesser role in the late 1980s, Magic has taken a more prominent role in the Laker offense. And, as usual, he has come through with flying colors.*

OPPOSITE: *Detroit's Isiah Thomas may not stand tall, but he sure plays tall. One of the NBA's best, Isiah directs the Piston's attack and has been an All-Star since he came to the NBA from Indiana, which he led to an NCAA title. He hopes the same is in the cards for the Pistons.*

ABOVE: *The spectacular Dominique Wilkins of Atlanta is known as "the human highlight film."*

RIGHT: *The latest candidate for "best ever" may be young Michael Jordan (23) of the Chicago Bulls. Air Jordan is a nearly unstoppable scorer.*

tainly are of championship caliber. But, as always, it takes a team to win it all, and in the 1980s it's mostly been the Lakers and Celtics at the head of the class.

The NBA has also bounced back, in the sense that the sport has come out of the funk of the mid to late 1970s. Most of the players are very competitive. The example set by Bird and Johnson seems to have taken hold all round the league. Or maybe it's chasing those two that has motivated many of the others.

By putting only top games on national television, then the playoffs, the league has also brought its ratings up. No more overkill. No more dull games between two mediocre teams. Only the best, and the best is still the greatest basketball in the world.

Bigger, better, faster, stronger. This describes the pro player of today. Not that the Robertsons, Wests and Baylors couldn't compete. They could, and so could the Schayes, Pettits and Cousys. But on the whole, the NBA is reaching new heights. And the league is for everyone, if they're good enough. Magic Johnson is a six-foot, nine-inch guard who can do it all, but in 1987-88 there is a rookie guard for the Washington Bullets named Tyrone Bogues who stands just five feet, three inches tall.

And some of today's players are spectacularly exciting. Dominique Wilkins of the Hawks is called the "Human Highlight Film" because of the way he flies through the air, making seemingly impossible shots and hair-raising slam dunks. Yet Wilkins is also becoming a total team player as the Hawks evolve as one of the better teams in the league.

Then there is Michael Jordan of the Chicago Bulls. He has revived a sagging franchise in a major market area. Nicknamed "Air Jordan," this product of North Carolina was the league's scoring champion in 1986-87, with a 37.1 average. And many of his shots bring the fans screaming to their feet. He, too, is already considered by many people to be an all-time great.

The league has also begun to showcase its great talents. The annual NBA All-Star Game now has several special features. There is an old-timers game, which allows fans to see some of their favorites from the recent past in action once more. And there are specialty events, such as a slam dunk contest and three-point range shooting contest. Jordan and Wilkins have dominated the slam dunk competition in recent years, though just a few years ago it was won by five-foot, seven-inch Spud Webb. And Larry Bird, with all his versatility, has seemingly cornered the market on the long-range shooting contest. Always the competitor, Bird comes to win.

But those are incidentals. In the end it's still the game that counts, that simple game of throwing a ball through a basket, the game that James Naismith invented so that youngsters would have some winter recreation. It certainly has come a long way, ascending to new heights in the 1980s, at both the college and the professional levels. The pioneer players did their jobs well, and the present-day players have carried on the tradition. Thanks to them all, we now never need to hesitate about using the adjective "great" when speaking about the game of basketball.

LEFT: *Pro basketball has come a long way from its early days, when the sport has to struggle for respectability. Now the game is bigger than ever, and the players are the best they've ever been. With players such as Larry Bird leading the way into the 1990s, the future looks very bright indeed.*

INDEX